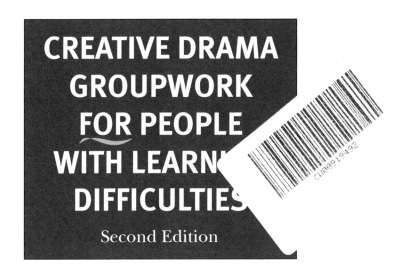

# CREATIVE DRAMA GROUPWORK FOR PEOPLE WITH LEARNING DIFFICULTIES

## Second Edition

The revised second edition of this practical manual is filled with easy-to-follow exercises and activities designed to facilitate creative drama sessions for people with learning difficulties. The activities in this book bring together music, theatre, movement and storytelling to not only develop fun and engaging group sessions, but to build confidence, increase self-esteem, and develop social and emotional awareness in group members. Highly sensitive to the range of learning needs and physical abilities of group members, the activities have been created to be engaging for a broad range of individuals regardless of age and ability, and can be adapted for use in a multitude of sectors such as education, psychology and speech and language therapy.

Key features of this edition include:

- New chapters exploring mindfulness and the importance of reflection
- Fully photocopiable resources including a session notes template to evaluate the impact of the creative drama group and collect useful data for the writing of reports
- Activities organised around key elements of creative drama, such as sensory work, life skills role-play, improvisation and de-roling

With its wealth of guidance, practical and adaptable activities and easy-to-follow structure, this is an invaluable resource for anybody leading or supporting children, young people and adults in creative drama.

**Anna Chesner** is co-director of the London Centre for Psychodrama Group and Individual Psychotherapy. She has a background in drama and drama teaching. She is a trained dramatherapist, with subsequent trainings in psychodrama and group analytic psychotherapy. She has worked in the NHS, Prison Service and in Private Practice. Anna runs workshops and training in London and internationally.

"Whether new to running drama groups or an experienced drama professional this book is both useful and practical. It gives a valuable introduction to the challenges of working creatively with people with learning disabilities, followed by a structured series of chapters which provide a wealth of warmup activities, games, drama exercises, improvisations and stories to use on a on-going basis. Anna Chesner brings her many years of practical knowledge, skill and expertise into a highly practical book that can be used by practitioners from a range of backgrounds in all kinds of community settings."

*Dr Clive Holmwood, Department of Therapeutic Arts,*
*University of Derby*

"It is very important that this book is available to contemporary teachers, practitioners and parents. The book sparkles with energy and imagination. A gift to us all as we work against cuts and a lack of resources. It is a sustainable book and a beam of light in our practice."

*Prof. Dr Sue Jennings, Distinguished Scholar*
*University of the Witwatersrand*

# CREATIVE DRAMA GROUPWORK FOR PEOPLE WITH LEARNING DIFFICULTIES

## Second Edition

*Anna Chesner*

Routledge
Taylor & Francis Group

LONDON AND NEW YORK

Second edition published 2020
by Routledge
2 Park Square, Milton Park, Abingdon, Oxon, OX14 4RN

and by Routledge
52 Vanderbilt Avenue, New York, NY 10017

*Routledge is an imprint of the Taylor & Francis Group, an informa business*

First edition published by Speechmark 1998

*British Library Cataloguing-in-Publication Data*
A catalogue record for this book is available from the British Library

*Library of Congress Cataloging-in-Publication Data*
A catalog record has been requested for this book

ISBN: 978-1-138-59694-8 (pbk)
ISBN: 978-0-429-48618-0 (ebk)

Typeset in ITC New Baskerville
by Servis Filmsetting Ltd, Stockport, Cheshire

# Contents

# Contents

••••••••••••••••••••••••••••••••••••••••••••••••••••

*continued from previous page*

# Acknowledgements

Thanks to the many service users and colleagues in Epsom & Mid Surrey, with whom I worked and learned in action from 1990 to 1995 and to Beverley Rees and Tae Catford who have both shared material with me in preparation for the second edition.

# Preface to the second edition

It is 21 years since the publication of the first edition of *Groupwork with Learning Disabilities: Creative Drama*. The book was well-received and has been translated into Italian and Hebrew.

Having been invited to update and revise the book for Routledge, it has been an interesting process to reflect on what changes need to be made in order to bring it up to date. I stand by the main thrust of the work in terms of session structure and principles of working with drama and many of the exercises and structures remain unchanged.

There are some changes to this edition. The title has been changed to reflect current usage and sensibilities. I have included some reflections on mindfulness – a practice I had been involved in at the time of writing the first edition, and which has now achieved mainstream recognition within the fields of health and education. I am pleased to be able to make some links within this edition.

I have made some small adjustments to the text in line with changes in our digital and diversity-aware age and have added an extra story in the Fairy Tales and Myths section for dramatization.

I have also included some structures for evaluating and assessing the work and creating an evidence base, which I hope will play their part in keeping a place for creative drama within the services provided for this user group.

August 2019

# Introduction

This book is intended for a wide public: not only for specialist dramatherapists, but for teachers, social workers, psychologists, speech and language therapists, group leaders, care workers, community workers and volunteers who are interested in the value and process of creativity and drama, and who have the opportunity to facilitate such work with people with learning difficulties.

It can be a daunting task to embark on a new method of working, or to work with a new client group, and many a drama project launched with the best of intentions has run aground through a lack of basic guidance and appropriate structure. This book offers some basic principles of working, a variety of approaches to drama and a number of specific drama structures to be used, adapted and added to as the work gets under way.

## The value of creative drama for people with learning difficulties

One of the privileges of being human is our capacity for creativity. This begins in earliest childhood and continues in some form throughout life. People with learning difficulties are no exception to this; nor are the staff and carers who work with them. Our creative ability may be highly developed or a largely unexplored potential. The art and craft of drama can help us discover and enjoy the power of our own creativity and playfulness within the context of a group.

Perhaps the most important reason to do creative drama is that it is fun. As an added bonus, it may bring about important benefits. The potential benefits of creative drama for people with learning difficulties are extensive, varying according to the individual membership, and the context and goals of the group. They include benefits for the individual and for the group. For example:

1 helping a group to bond,

2 increasing tolerance, respect and understanding between group members,

3 enhancing individual self-esteem and the confidence to communicate,

# Introduction

continued from previous page

4 increasing the awareness and appreciation of boundaries, physical, social and emotional,

5 developing social skills,

6 developing physical skills,

7 developing verbal skills,

8 developing assertiveness, self-advocacy and life skills,

9 developing spontaneity,

10 enhancing the ability to make choices,

11 developing the imagination and the ability to play,

12 learning about other people, places and times beyond the immediate here and now.

● As with any journey into new territory, some preliminary preparation is advisable. There are a number of questions it is useful to consider.

## How big should a creative drama group be?

There is no hard-and-fast rule about this. The larger a group is, the more autonomy and self-discipline the members will need. In a less able, more dependent or highly challenging group, a higher ratio of staff or helpers to group members is required to help the group to focus, and to offer support with specific difficulties, such as mobility, where necessary. It is worth erring on the side of caution in terms of keeping a group relatively small, and making use of available supportive colleagues, rather than letting a group flounder and succumb to chaos or frustration in its early days. A group of between three and five can be run as a small group, from six to 12 as a medium group, and above 12 should be considered a large group.

## How often and for how long should we meet?

There are a number of possible formats, and the work can be easily adapted to fit in with whichever is chosen. A weekly group of between one and two hours could be taken as a norm, the length of a session being a reflection of the ability of the group to sustain concentration. Once the length of time

# Introduction

is decided upon, it is preferable to stick to this so that the boundary of the work is clear and the group members know what to expect: when and where they meet, how long for and how often. It may be psychologically useful and administratively necessary to agree on the total duration of a sequence of sessions. I have found a short-term group of six to 10 weekly sessions to be an appropriate format for group and group leader to get a sense of the work. A longer-term weekly group allows members to develop confidence in the ways of working and to build on the skills mastered. Such a group may last a year or more. There may be external factors dictating the duration of a group, such as timetabling of other activities, availability of work space and so on. Within these limitations it is also worth considering internal factors when programming a creative drama group. For example, would the group benefit from the security of a regular long-term group, or would the idea of a long-term commitment be oppressive? Are there specific goals to be achieved that will require a generous amount of time?

Another groupwork model of working is the short-term intensive project. A group might meet together every morning, or every morning and afternoon for a few days, and work intensively together. This could be considered a kind of drama workshop holiday, and might be part of a residential field trip. The group may work towards the goal of sharing their work at the end of the project through a performance or open workshop.

## What kind of work space do we need?

### Size
Ideally, the room should be large enough to move in freely, without being so large that a group feels lost in it. If there is a lack of choice in terms of work space, consider matching the number of group members to the available space. Maximize space in a small room by clearing away as much unneeded furniture as possible. Consider the use of screens to divide a space that feels too large.

### Privacy
During the session the room should be used only for the creative drama work. This may mean negotiating with and educating people external to the group not to interrupt or disturb the work.

# Introduction

*continued from previous page*

## Contents

If the room has other functions, for example as a living room, a meeting room, a public hall or a recreation room, it may contain furniture not relevant to its use as a creative drama workshop space. In this case it is advisable to clear the space as much as possible before the start of the session. There are two reasons for this. Firstly, this puts the room 'in role' as the drama space, where different rules operate and where there are different expectations placed on group members. When the environment is returned to its former state, and it is in a sense 'de-roled', people will be expected to behave in it accordingly. Secondly, objects that may be damaged by the potential boisterousness of drama activity are protected, and group members themselves are protected both from possible damage to themselves and from the inhibition that comes from having to be concerned with protecting the surroundings.

## Equipment

Some basic equipment is extremely useful in providing the impetus for drama activities. This is especially true for people with learning difficulties, for whom concrete objects, which can be experienced with the senses, are more accessible than abstract ideas. A store of props can be built up over time, often without great expense. Particular props and equipment will be mentioned in the descriptions of each drama structure in the various chapters of the book. For an initial stock, consider acquiring some of the following.

- Balls of various colours, textures and sizes. (Rolled up socks can also be used.)

- Fabric of various textures, colours and sizes, from headscarf size to sarong or sheet.

- Hats, suggestive of different characters, gender and social functions (anything from a tiara to a policeman's helmet)

- Pictures of various sizes, from postcard to poster, which suggest a variety of subjects and mood.

- Musical instruments and facilities for playing and making recorded music or sound effects.

# Introduction

Many everyday objects can also be of value in drama, whether they are to be used according to their usual function or in a new and imaginative way (for example, a wooden spoon can be used as a cooking utensil or as a magic wand, a microphone or the head and body of a puppet).

## Who should join a creative drama group?

When a group has a balanced composition and 'gels', it is a particularly satisfying experience for all participants. Exactly what makes a group of people compatible is hard to say. In the early stages of a group there is often a period of testing out of self, peers and group leaders. At this time it may seem that the group is not in balance. However, it is wise to allow some time for the group to find its own balance, rather than judging it too hastily as 'difficult' or 'not workable'. The negotiating for power and status, and the testing of boundaries, is usually a healthy and necessary preliminary stage of the work. It is not necessary for everyone in a creative drama group to like each other. Indeed, some difference of opinion and personality can add to the creative potential of the group. Individuals perceived as 'challenging', 'demanding' or difficult' can be accepted and incorporated into a group if this preliminary stage is handled with clarity and sensitivity. When such individuals feel themselves accepted and appreciated by a group, their self-esteem rises, and the experience of surviving and transforming a difficult situation is therapeutic for the individuals and the group as a whole. Too much personal antagonism, on the other hand, can be a problem and there is a limit to the amount of friction and difficulty a group can tolerate. A group must be able to feel safe together, so a basic level of goodwill between group members certainly helps.

It is also worth looking at the gender balance of a group. Single-gender groups can work well, as can mixed groups. As a general rule of thumb, if the group is a mixed gender group the numbers of each gender should be similar. A single representative of one gender should be avoided if possible, as this person may feel isolated or outnumbered. Sometimes the collective personality or presence of one gender is particularly forceful in a group, in which case an awareness of this factor may help in choosing suitable members of the opposite gender.

# Introduction

continued from previous page

The creative drama group can be an enjoyable experience for the less expressive members of a community as well as for known extroverts and obvious 'performers'. The use of dramatic structures to contain and guide communication possibilities can be liberating for the shy group member, while providing useful boundaries for more dominant group members. The levels of visible engagement in the group may be different for each participant. The creative drama group can provide a valuable sense of belonging for those whose participation is perhaps more reserved. A variety of personality types tends to enrich the membership.

## What qualities are needed by the group leader/s?

### A playful confidence and a confident playfulness

● The leader's own relationship with the activities she suggests has a profound influence on the ability and willingness of group members to enter into the work in a relaxed and enthusiastic way. In this respect the worst attitude is one of embarrassment, with the implicit message to the group: "Relax, play, perform, but don't expect me to." A group is encouraged by the enjoyment and enthusiasm of a group leader who is happy to have a go herself, to play seriously and to care about the dramatic play of the group. The implicit message she gives is more of an invitation: "Let's try this. Join me."

### Clarity of intention and communication

● When introducing the work, consider the ability of the group to understand. Explain structures a step at a time, and be prepared to take a step backwards or to go more slowly. Explain through example, by modelling a particular exercise or part exercise. It is often easier to show what you mean than to explain verbally. Try rehearsing how you will explain something beforehand, so that your attention during the session can be on really communicating rather than on looking for words. If a structure is new to you, try it out in some form for yourself first, so that you can be clear about what you are asking of people, and why.

### Flexibility

● One of the joys of leading a creative drama group is that it is full of surprises. The creative response of the group will often be quite different from your own expectations. The ability to incorporate new ideas and

# Introduction

new interpretations of the group into the framework of the session will greatly enhance the work. The level of control appropriate to leading a creative drama group is one that gives a feeling of safety, containment and sufficient guidance while valuing the spontaneous contributions of group members.

## A note on multiple difficulties and special needs

Each individual has their own unique combination of ability and difficulties. For this reason I have not specified particular structures for particular difficulties. The creative drama group is a place for participants to try things out safely and discover their own abilities, limitations and preferences. Most structures offered in this book can be adapted to suit individual needs. Participants engage with suggested structures in their own way and at their own level. An interesting group activity can give a strong incentive for individuals and the group to find creative ways to ensure that everyone finds a way to participate according to their own ability.

Creative drama structures can elicit strong responses in group members, who may be put in touch with difficult memories, wounds or traumas by activities and processes in the drama group. It is important for the group leader, whether trained in a therapeutic discipline or not, to be sensitive to this possibility with all group members, including those whose verbal communication is limited. The norms of physical contact and proximity are different during a creative drama session and many participants will understand this implicitly. Touch and contact must be contracted for and consent given. This may need to be done non-verbally, so facilitators need to keep a vigilant eye on where each person's boundaries are in relation to this. At the end of the session, usual boundaries must be clearly re-established between group members and between group leaders and group members. This issue should be addressed explicitly in the group. The transitions into and out of a session will also be facilitated by consistent adherence to the five-phase session structure described below.

It is important that physical contact be mutually acceptable and that participants are supported in their right to refuse activities which are unacceptable to them. (See, in particular, *Chapter 2.*)

# Introduction

continued from previous page

## A note on the age of group members

The activities in this book can be suitable for both adults and children. It is left to the group leader to choose activities that are thematically relevant and acceptable to the particular group membership, and to present them in a way that is accessible and respectful to the individuals in the drama group. In recent years, there has been great emphasis placed on the concept of 'age appropriateness' in the field of learning difficulties, with mixed results. There certainly is a place for this concept in the creative drama group, but a subtle one. Play, creativity and spontaneity are appropriate and meaningful at every age. Adults should of course nonetheless be treated as adults.

## A note on gender

Assume that both drama workers and participants in groups can be of either gender. I have written of the group leader as 'she', by which is to be understood 'she, he or they'. In writing about participants I have used both male and female examples. In each case the participant could equally well be of the opposite gender.

## Structuring a session

### Form and freedom

The dual concept of *form and freedom* is at the heart of the dramatic process. Form concerns itself with the shape of each activity, whether an individual exercise within the creative drama session, or the session as a whole. Freedom in this sense is the spirit of the work. It is the freedom to express, to respond to form, to play and to create. The relationship of dramatic form to create freedom is an intimate one. Using the metaphor of a house, form provides the basic architectural design, and the bricks and mortar out of which the building is constructed. What happens within the building is partly conditioned by its structure, and is also a matter of individual responses and contributions of those inside it.

Within the drama session, form provides essential safety and structure, without which there is the danger that freedom will degenerate into uncontained chaos. Form gives an element of the known, within which

# Introduction

and in response to which the group is invited to try something new to the moment, drawing freely on its spontaneity. Each new creative contribution has the possibility of inspiring a further creative response within the group. The potential for free expression within a drama group is vast. There is a corresponding necessity for clear, containing structure.

## Five-phase session design

We will be looking at specific structures of work that can form a smaller or greater part of a creative drama session. These are intended for use within a balanced session, that is a session with form. Some structures are more suited to one phase of a session, other structures to another phase. There follows a basic five-phase design for the creative drama session (see *Figure 1*). This design forms the skeleton of each session, and can be fleshed out in a different way each session, through a variety of different structures.

Phase 1: Arrivals and greetings (see *Chapter 1*).
Phase 2: Warming up to the space, to each other and to the work (see *Chapters 2, 3, 4* and *6*).
Phase 3: Development: the central focus of the session (see any of the above chapters and also *Chapters 3–9*).
Phase 4: Distancing and de-roling (see *Chapter 12*).
Phase 5: Goodbyes and departures (see *Chapter 13*).

This five-phase process ensures that the group has time to ease into a session, and time to ease out again. The most intense or complex period of activity and concentration is designed to come in the middle of the session. This is the point at which the group is most likely to explore an imaginary world through enactment. An activity of this kind involves an agreement as a group to participate in the 'as if' of a make-believe world. This 'willing suspension of disbelief' is at the heart of play and drama, a marked stepping away from concrete everyday reality into a state where all things could be possible. There is a necessary build-up towards this point, in phases one and two, and a gradual letting go of the work afterwards, in phases four and five.

By consistently following the five-phase process, the creative drama sessions will have an underlying rhythm and shape, which gives a feeling

# Introduction

*continued from previous page*

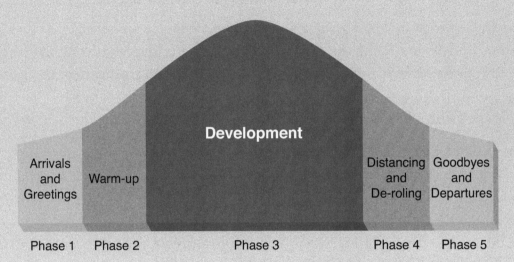

*Figure 1* Five-phase session structure

of familiarity to group members and a sense of security to the group and group leaders. It is advisable for the group leader to plan the structural skeleton of a session in advance with this five-part format in mind. As the group adds to the structure spontaneously, there will often be changes to the plan, but the group leader can keep in touch with the overall rhythm of the session, ensuring that there is an easeful journey into and out of the dramatic work.

## Levels of challenge

Many of the structures described in this book can be used either as warm-ups or as the central development of the session, depending on the level of experience and confidence in the group. An important task of the group leader is to be sensitive to the level of challenge appropriate to a particular group at a particular time. A group that is just starting to work together, and for whom the language of drama is a relatively new one, will appreciate the chance to master simple structures and to return to familiar ground. A group that has worked together for a longer period, or whose members have extensive drama experience, may be more able to develop and enhance the structures offered by the group leader, and may be ready for more challenge in the central development phase of the session. The level of complexity and challenge needs to be gauged also according to the mood of a group on a particular day, as well as the level of ability of group members to understand, to co-operate with each other, to initiate and to sustain interest. Many structures are described both in their simplest form and with variations of increasing complexity.

# Introduction

## Helping the helpers help

Many creative drama groups will benefit from a team approach. While the leadership of the group should be clear – perhaps one person or a pair of leaders – having helpers alongside can be an essential support. Some participants require help with mobility, others with emotional management. It is vital that there be a positive relationship between the leadership and the helpers. Ideally the helpers will be consistent attenders, who get to know the culture of the group and are able to respect the different norms that are in place during a creative drama activity. Helpers may need an induction and ongoing reminders about these key concepts:

### Patience and process

In many areas of life the pragmatic perspective of needing to get something done may lead support workers to take over a task from someone with a learning difficulty, to hurry them along, or become impatient with them. While this is understandable it goes against the purpose of a creative drama group where the emphasis is on process rather than product. An example might be a participant who is reluctant to join the circle at the start of a session. Within a creative drama session, encouragement will be balanced by respect for the difficulty. It may be several sessions before this person joins the circle at the start of the group, along with their peers. Of course this could be speeded up by a helper or leader taking a firm stance from day one, but there is a higher value in facilitating a genuine choice over time, and this requires patience.

### Exploration and autonomy

Similarly, within an exercise or activity the principle would be to offer support in taking a small step rather than staff taking over in order to get a quicker or better result. It is important that all staff resist any punitive or over-controlling tendency to managing difficulty, whilst holding the boundaries of keeping everyone safe.

### Staying present

Change may be slow, and the group structure may seem repetitive. Helpers may find themselves wanting to get on with an administrative or practical task of their own. However, if they are able to stay present to the current

# Introduction

continued from previous page

focus this will be of immense support to the participants and the group leader/s. They are role models of active participation and attentiveness. See section on mindfulness below.

### Potential to bring own creativity

The split between 'client' and 'staff' or between leaders and helpers can be minimized if helpers also bring their own creativity and talents to the drama group. At the appropriate moments, sharing these skills helps to create human to human bonds that may also have positive repercussions in the relationship outside of the group. Of course, these contributions need to be made within the overall structure of the session. With this in mind, leaders should pay attention to the skills and creative interests of all who are present in the group.

### Different relationship norms

The five-phase session structure helps to mark the creative drama group as a place where there are different relationship norms than in the classroom, workplace or home environment – the group is a place for sharing, playfulness and experimentation.

## Creative drama and mindfulness

Mindfulness is the practice of focussing attention. It originates in Buddhist meditation practices, and is increasingly used to help empower clients with physical pain or mental health difficulties to manage their condition, to 'come to their senses'.

Training in mindfulness for the general population might include focusing on the breath, particularly the sensation of the breath moving in and out of the nose, or the rise and fall of the breath in the chest or belly. In addition, there are activities such as scanning, whereby the practitioner puts attention into different parts of the body and notices the sensations present.

These activities can create a sense of being grounded, calm and present in the moment. The more we are present in the moment and grounded in the here and now sensation of our being, the less energy seems to go into obsessive thinking, or automatic patterns of thought and behaviour.

# Introduction

Traditional training in mindfulness tends to focus on the individual's internal experience, which is quite a subtle thing to attend to. It is therefore more readily accessible to those who have a certain capacity to contain themselves, to reflect, and to bear to be present to their own thoughts and feelings, which may at times be disturbing or unpleasant.

Creative drama is interactive, action-based, structured and fun. It engages the body, and therefore the breath. It involves movement, the senses, and mental activity such as imagination and concentration. For this reason, many activities in this book have the capacity to create a degree of mindful attention in both the group leaders and the participants. Let us consider how this happens.

Simple, repetitive structures are practised in the group. These involve engaging the body in an intentional way. This in turn has an impact on the breath, which may become more full, rhythmic or calmer depending on the activity. There is also the adherence to a simple rule or sequence. These structures or activities require just enough attention to be absorbing – but not so much that the participants are overwhelmed or find themselves drifting off. Even if the attention wanders a little, the structure is there for them to come back to. Instructions include where to direct our focus – whether listening to a fellow group member talking, during a turn-taking round; directing our gaze towards a particular person or object; or the physical sensation of all stamping our feet on the floor or squeezing our neighbours' hands.

The absorption that arises from these activities leads to an increase in mindful presence.

An additional benefit comes from the experience of mastery. When an activity which is at first challenging, becomes familiar, there is a pleasure in doing it and knowing that we can do it.

It is therefore very helpful for the group facilitators to notice the **quality of attention** that is present in the group, and in the individual group members, including your own. If someone becomes disturbed or disturbing in the group, over-excited or distressed, try using a gentle reminder of what the

# Introduction

continued from previous page

current activity is to focus their attention back to the here and now activity. At moments such as this we are trying to down-regulate their stress response, and in order to do that we need to contain and down-regulate our own potential frustration as a group facilitator. In this way our own mindfulness creates the conditions for an increased degree of mindfulness in the group members.

# Overview

In this book you will find various drama structures grouped in chapters around a particular focus. There follows a brief overview of these chapters and the rationale behind them. For the possible placing of each chapter within the five-phase session plan, please refer to *Figure 2*.

## Arrivals and greetings

What does it mean to arrive at a creative drama group? On the one hand, it is a temporary leaving behind of the everyday way of being together. On the other hand, it is an arrival in a special space, where something new and creative can take place.

The first minutes should take both these perspectives into account. The beginning of a session is a transitional period, a space between two kinds of activity and ways of being. As such, it is full of potential, and for this very reason can also be scary. It is reassuring for a group if this part of the session has a strong component of familiarity and ritual. All the structures in this chapter have the group sitting in a circle at the beginning of a session, which is both containing and relational.

## Body work

The ability to move expressively is a core drama skill. Exercises to increase the expressive movement repertoire can be seen both as training for role-play and improvisation and as creative drama experiences in their own right. In everyday life the range of movements we need to use is limited and, unless we are in pain, there is a tendency to give the body and its movement potential little attention. People with learning difficulties who tend to be more dependent on others often use an even more limited range of movements. The exercises described in this chapter give participants a structured opportunity to wake up to their body and 'get in touch with themselves' physically.

You can compile a movement warm-up out of a selection of these structures. Over a period of sessions, try using a combination of familiar and new structures. The familiar ones give the opportunity of mastery, while the new ones bring an element of challenge and variety to a movement or warm-up programme. All may lead to an increase in mindful presence.

# Overview

● ● ● ● ● ● ● ● ● ● ● ● ● ● ● ● ● ● ● ● ● ● ● ● ● ● ● ● ● ● ● ● ● ● ● ● ● ● ● ● ● ● ● ●

*continued from previous page*

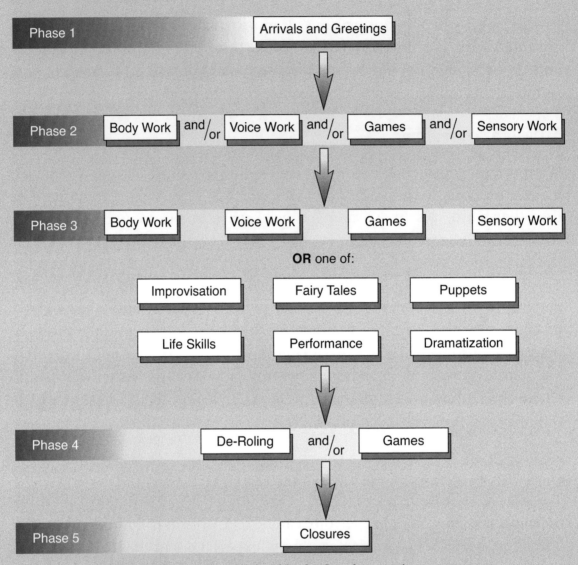

| Phase 1 | Arrivals and Greetings |
|---|---|

| Phase 2 | Body Work | and/or | Voice Work | and/or | Games | and/or | Sensory Work |

| Phase 3 | Body Work | Voice Work | Games | Sensory Work |

**OR** one of:

| Improvisation | Fairy Tales | Puppets |
|---|---|---|
| Life Skills | Performance | Dramatization |

| Phase 4 | De-Roling | and/or | Games |

| Phase 5 | Closures |

*Figure 2* Choice of material within the five-phase session structure

## Sensory work

Drama can be used to help people with learning difficulties enjoy their senses and increase their sensory awareness. This helps them to feel more 'grounded', aware and centred in their body and more connected to the world around them, to become more mindfully present. The structures in this chapter include games, movement work and improvisation, which could belong equally well in other chapters. They are brought together here because of their common emphasis on the world of the senses. You can use these structures to develop trust and playfulness in the early phases of a group, or as the central focus for a series of sessions.

# Overview

## Voice work

Many people with learning difficulties lack confidence in their own ability to express themselves in words and with the voice. This can result in shyness and in stereotypic, unvaried patterns when using the voice. Small, simple exercises approached within the framework of a creative drama group give an opportunity to play with the possibilities of the voice. With practice, voice work can help improve communication skills by giving time to work on listening skills, making sounds and being heard. Voice work is a physical activity and brings benefits in terms of relaxation. The work focuses on the breath, head, throat and upper body in particular. The element of vibration acts like an internal massage, giving a sense of space and ease within the body and again linking helpfully to the potential for mindful presence.

Using the voice in unusual ways can be fun. Babies naturally experiment freely with their voices, to great effect. As we grow up we learn to limit the full natural potential of the voice for the sake of social convention. If the group leader or team of helpers are inhibited themselves in using their voices it is advisable to practise alone before presenting voice structures to a group.

The voice exercises in this chapter can be used as the central focus for a series of creative drama sessions, as part of a process of preparation for a performance project, or as an occasional element within the warm-up or development phase of the creative drama group.

## Life skills role-play

The creative drama group can be used as a space to rehearse real life situations. The danger of 'making a mistake' is minimized in the drama situation, as it is 'not real' in a very liberating way. The roles and lessons learned within the semi-reality of the creative drama situation often have important applications in real life.

Life skills role-play is of particular relevance to people with learning difficulties, who may lack experience and confidence in situations most people take for granted. Within the creative drama sessions they can build up confidence by trying things out beforehand.

# Overview

continued from previous page

This chapter includes guidelines for warming the group up for life skills role-play sessions, as well as sample scenarios of particular everyday situations.

## Games

Games are an important part of creative drama work. They are a good example of the combination of form and freedom in drama. There are clear rules to be followed, which can be very simple. Within these rules there is the opportunity for playful experimentation and a sense of contributing to a whole group experience. They can provide containment for rowdier group members and encouragement for the more reticent.

Games can form the central development of a session, or be used as a warm-up for more free dramatic expression. They are an enjoyable way to learn to co-operate in a group; even competitive games require a high degree of co-operation. The ability to work and play together is essential for imaginative drama activity as well as for satisfaction in life.

## Puppets

Puppets can be an absorbing tool for creating stories and dramatic play. They can create an important sense of distance for those who find direct interpersonal interaction threatening. In puppet play there is a tacit agreement to communicate at one remove, through the medium of the puppets. So for those people with learning difficulties whose shyness inhibits them in more direct creative drama work, puppet play may open up a new possibility. The puppet has a character and apparent life of its own, but a life that is dormant until activated by a human hand or voice. This paradoxical process is fascinating. The experience of giving animation to the puppet by holding or moving it is an empowering one. Those for whom active participation, even in puppet play, is too demanding may also be drawn into the puppet drama from the position of interested spectator.

In this chapter various kinds of puppets are described, and there are suggestions as to their use.

# Overview

## Improvisation

Improvisation can be a particularly rewarding dramatic activity. It gives participants the chance to exercise their spontaneity and creativity. Improvisation is fun, and at the same time builds confidence that is useful in everyday life. In terms of form and freedom, improvisation gives participants a relatively free rein to explore and develop their own ideas. As a group activity, it depends on sensitivity and awareness amongst group members.

Many exercises and structures throughout this book use elements of improvisation, and can help a group build up a repertoire of improvisation skills. This chapter includes three preparatory exercises for introducing the idea and basic skills of improvisation. Subsequent exercises offer various starting points for improvisation: some use the question 'Where?' others use the question 'Who?' How these starting points are picked up and developed by a particular group at a given moment will vary. In other words, the 'What happens?' is left open. The unknown that gradually unfolds is the unique quality of improvisation.

## Dramatization

The focus for dramatization can come from a fictional source such as a known story, poem, play, song or film, or from a real life source, such as current affairs, the personal stories of group members, the history of the group, its present dynamic or choices it needs to make. This chapter gives examples of possible approaches to each of these sources.

Before any enactment, give the group members an opportunity to warm up to each other and to being in the group (see *Chapters 1, 2* and *6*). Similarly, allow adequate time for de-roling, reflecting and returning to the here and now at the end of an enactment (see *Chapters 12* and *13*).

## Fairy tales and myths

Fairy tales and myths can be enacted by creative drama groups of all ages. We respond differently to fairy tales and myths at different stages of personal development, and they can be appreciated at many different levels.

# Overview

continued from previous page

When exploring fairy tales and myths dramatically with people with learning difficulties, it is useful to break the story up into manageable scenes. Each scene of the story can be read or told briefly and simply, and then enacted. The fairy tale or myth can provide a framework for a dramatic project lasting several sessions. If you use it in this way, remember to begin each session by recapping the story so far, perhaps even repeating a short enactment from the previous session. Also allow sufficient time at the end of each session for de-roling. This can be done by dismantling the scenery, removing costumes and props, and spending time together as a group in the here and now. The characters and story are put away symbolically until the next drama session.

Since fairy tales and myths contain 'good' and 'bad' characters, boldly depicted, it is especially important in the de-roling to emphasize the distinction between the character played and the person playing it. This can be done by literally saying "goodbye" to the character while putting away the costume or prop belonging to the character. The group leader and group members can welcome each other by name as each person leaves the enactment and returns clearly to the here and now, saying, for example, "Goodbye, witch! Until next time! Hello Peter, welcome back!"

The question of who plays which role can be negotiated each session, so that no-one gets stuck with a role that they are uncomfortable with, and so that several people may get the chance to play a sought-after role. If there is no volunteer for a particular role, which may happen initially in the case of 'baddies', one of the group leaders can play that role, either alone or as a supportive double alongside a group member who is prepared to try it. It is important not to push anyone into a negatively perceived role. These roles offer wonderful dramatic scope, and when group members see how much fun they are to play they may be encouraged to volunteer another time.

This chapter includes two shorter tales, *The Three Wishes* and *Goldilocks and the Three Bears*, which could be manageable as single session activities. There then follow three longer fairy stories: *The Frog Prince, Hansel and Gretel* and the Greek myth of *Demeter and Persephone*. I have retold these with a simplified narrative and broken them down into dramatic scenes, with suggestions for

# Overview

possible roles and approaches to enactment. Different groups may be able to manage one or more scenes in each session. At the end of a project, when each scene has been explored individually, it is satisfying to enact the whole fairy tale or myth in one piece, with a short narrative linking the scenes.

## Performance

There are pros and cons to performance work in the context of the creative drama group. Performance is very much an optional extra to creative drama work. For many drama workers it is the here and now experience in the group which matters, and the idea of performance is tainted with associations of achievement. The creative drama process is enough in itself, without needing to lead to a product. Current approaches to people with learning difficulties are perhaps too goal-oriented already, as witnessed by the common term for day activities, 'training'. The creative drama group can be a space with different, less achievement driven values.

There are equally strong arguments for performance work. Performance gives the creative drama work a moment of completion. A performance project does not stretch into an indefinite future. There is a reason for the work: the show must go on, and it must be ready at the agreed time. Individuals and the group as a whole can feel proud of their creative product. Perhaps most importantly, performance requires an audience, a group of people whose role is to watch and to listen. The performance is both a gift to the audience and an invitation for that audience to appreciate the performers.

In previous chapters there are numerous structures which have the potential to be developed into performance projects. The decision as to whether to follow that route is an important one and must involve all group members as well as the group leader. In making the decision, there are several factors to be borne in mind. There is often less immediate personal gratification for participants during a rehearsal process than during a regular creative drama session. A performance project requires a significant degree of co-operation and self-discipline. Sometimes it is important to stick with something difficult and work on it, rather than move on to something new. One or two group

# Overview

continued from previous page

members who lack these skills can be 'carried' and contained by the rest of the group. The majority must be well motivated, however, and able on occasion to take a back seat personally for the sake of the group or the show. The fact of the impending performance may act as an inspiration to acquire and refine these group skills.

This chapter looks at different models of performance projects and gives guidance on the processes of decision making and preparation.

## De-roling

De-roling means consciously letting go of an imaginary role. It is an important stage of the creative drama process, used at the end of an enactment, often towards the end of a session. Before asking participants to take on roles, it is worth giving consideration to the subsequent process of de-roling and to familiarize yourself with a few simple de-roling techniques.

When we play a role in a creative drama activity we embody that role. We hold a sense of the role in the imagination and express its being physically and vocally. This is a powerful process and one which we engage with at many levels. At one level, we know that the role is 'not me' and that we are 'just playing'. At the same time, we 'enter into' that role and to some extent leave our everyday familiar role behind. De-roling facilitates leaving the imaginary role behind sufficiently for us to be able to return to our own sense of self.

In children's spontaneous dramatic play the process happens tacitly without the need for a particular structure. In a creative drama group, however, different participants may identify with imaginary roles to differing degrees and the group leader has the responsibility of providing safety and clarity. Formalized de-roling is part of this responsibility; it is particularly important for people with learning difficulties, for whom the boundary between 'I' and 'not I' may be less stable.

In terms of managing a lively group, de-roling helps the group leader control the excitement level in a group and to bring mindful focus and concentration into the here and now.

# Overview

In this chapter there are physical and reflection-based structures for de-roling.

## Closures

The final moments of the creative drama group are a time for the individuals to take leave of the group and of the creative drama context. The process should be clearly marked so that participants can prepare themselves to face the familiar reality outside the drama space, with its demands and life roles.

This chapter includes some simple suggestions for ritualizing this process of transition.

## Evaluation and creating an evidence base

In this chapter you will find some suggestions for evaluating the impact of the creative drama group and collecting data for use in report writing.

# Arrivals
# and
# Greetings

# Coming together

## Preparation

A circle of chairs, bean bags or cushions is laid out in the drama work space. Include an appropriate space for each wheelchair user. There should be a defined place for each group member, including group leaders and helpers.

## Activity

As each person arrives they join the circle, perhaps after hanging up their coats, going to the toilet and so on.

## Purpose

This structure is particularly useful if group members arrive for the session separately and over a period of a few minutes. If possible, the group leader should already be sitting as each person arrives. There is a clear focus in the space and a place to experience the coming together of the group. The activity of waiting is given a structure, and the moment when the group is complete is visible and clear. This moment is anticipated by those already in the circle, and helps to give a sense of group identity.

## Further development

1 Informal discussion. It is natural, while sitting waiting for the group to begin, to share any news informally, or to talk about hopes and fears for the coming session.

2 The group leader can also ask specific questions or make specific comments relating to the here and now situation of waiting and arrivals, such as "Who's here?", "Who are we waiting for?" or "Who is absent?"

3 It is interesting to notice who sits where in the group. Do some group members always choose to sit next to or opposite the same person? Over a longer period of time, do they become more flexible or more assertive about these choices? **NB** This level of change tends to happen very slowly, so you may wish to include observations such as these when taking notes after sessions. Such notes contribute to evaluation and building an evidence base (see *Chapter 14*).

# Who's here?

## Activity

The group leader invites everybody to look around the circle and take a moment to notice who is in the group. Each person (including the group leader) then takes it in turn to introduce themselves to the group, by saying their name or signing, or making a gesture of introduction.

## Purpose

The exercise is a simple ritual in which each person is the focus of attention for a short moment, and is seen and heard by the group. It serves as a reminder of the membership and identity of the group. It introduces the idea of turn-taking early on in the session. It involves both active and passive participation as each person makes their personal contribution to the round and also pays attention to the others in the group.

## Further development

1 The greeting. After each person says their name (or makes a gesture of arrival) the group responds with a greeting. For example:

- *Individual:* (I'm) Dev.
- *Group:* Hello/Good morning/Hi, Dev.

2 After the initial going around, the group leader asks if there is someone in the group who can remember everybody's name. A first volunteer stands and introduces each person; and receives praise or applause for the achievement. Other volunteers may also feel like having a go. If someone has difficulty in remembering, they can be encouraged to ask, "What's your name?", or other group members can help them out.

3 In a second going-round, each person is invited to say one other piece of information about themselves that they would like the group to know. This can be something factual, such as

"I'm Dev and live with my parents and sister", or something more related to feelings, such as

"I'm Dev and I feel sad today."

CREATIVE DRAMA GROUPWORK FOR PEOPLE WITH LEARNING DIFFICULTIES

# Hello song with handshake

## Activity

In this song a handshake is passed around the group. *A* shakes the hand of *B*, who then shakes *C*'s hand, and so on until the last person shakes *A*'s hand and the circle is complete. As each pair shakes hands the whole group sings a simple refrain that is repeated with each new name:

*Babs is shaking hands with Cheryl*
*Babs is shaking hands with Cheryl*
*Babs is shaking hands with Cheryl*
*It's good to see you here.*

*Cheryl's shaking hands with Dev,* and so on.

When the handshake has found its way all round the circle, all hold hands and sing together:

*We're all shaking hands together*
*We're all shaking hands together*
*We're all shaking hands together*
*It's good to see you here.*

Any tune that is easy to remember will work. If this activity becomes a regular structure, there will be plenty of opportunity for repetition and practice, so even slightly more difficult tunes can be mastered.

## Purpose

The song provides a ritualized form of greeting that soon becomes familiar in a group. Group members get to hear their own name sung and to practise the names of the other members of the group. Each person contributes to the whole ritual by receiving and giving a handshake. It tends to be popular with all age groups and creates a fun and friendly atmosphere at the start of a session. It helps to give people a chance to arrive and focus on being together in a mindful, present way.

# Hello song with handshake

*continued from previous page*

## Further development

1 Use the song to work on eye contact, encouraging each pair to give eye contact while shaking hands.

2 Ask for someone in the group to volunteer to begin the song and the handshake. This can provide group members with a framework for taking initiative and trying out a moment of leadership once they feel confident with the form.

# Hello circle song

## Activity

The group holds hands in a circle, takes a moment to look at each other, and sings:

> *We are a circle*
> *We are friends*
> *Sitting here together*
> *Holding hands.*
>
> *Hello Babs, hello Cheryl, hello Dev . . .*
> *Sitting here together*
> *Holding hands.*

## Purpose

This is an alternative to the handshake song above, useful for ringing the changes. The focus is more on the group as a whole. Each person's name is sung in turn by the whole group, while the circle of hands is maintained throughout the song. The continuous circle is particularly helpful for a sense of containment, wholeness and focus in a restless or anxious group.

## Further development

1 Instead of holding hands, everyone can clap hands together in an appropriate rhythm, and change the final line of both verses to 'Clapping hands'.

2 For a variation with more movement, change the last line of both verses to 'Waving hands'. Wave both hands in the air for the first verse; then wave alternately with left and right hand to each named individual in the second verse; and again with both hands and much energy for the last line.

3 Where direct physical contact is difficult, try using a circular communiband or long cloth, so that people can connect as a circle by each holding the cloth. In this way the connection is concretized and made visible and tangible, but without direct person to person touch.

# Simple ball hello game

## Preparation

Have a ball close at hand.

## Activity

The game is usually played while the group is seated in a circle at the beginning of the session, either as a first activity or after one of the opening rituals mentioned above. A ball is introduced into the circle, preferably one that is easy to hold and handle. A soft foam ball works well. Choose the size according to the physical abilities or difficulties of the group. The ball is passed or thrown to someone in the circle, following this sequence:

1 Make eye contact with the person you choose.
2 Call the name of the person you are sending the ball to.
3 Send the ball.

The recipient then chooses who to send the ball to next.

## Purpose

Each person has the experience of choosing someone to make contact with and being chosen. It is interesting to see if certain group members always choose each other, and whether they become more expansive with their range of choices over time. The game allows people to feel included, so if someone tends to get left out the group leader should keep an eye on this; and she can make sure they are included by throwing the ball to them.

## Further development

1 Once the basic game is mastered, try using a different ball each session, or changing to a different ball partway through. A large inflatable ball, or balloon, feels very different from a small beanbag or spidery rubber koosh ball. Some balls can be rolled across the floor rather than thrown.

2 To emphasize eye contact and non-verbal communication, include a few minutes during which the game is played in silence. This might involve an element of simple clowning, gesticulating wildly or pulling a face to make sure that the chosen person is ready to catch the ball.

3 Try using a whisper, or calling loudly (see *Chapter 4* on voice work).

CREATIVE DRAMA GROUPWORK FOR PEOPLE WITH LEARNING DIFFICULTIES

# News round

## Preparation

Have a prop to hand to represent a microphone or 'talking stick'. Suitable objects range from a wooden spoon to a maraca, clave or a real microphone.

## Activity

The talking stick is passed around or across the circle. Only the person who holds it can talk, while everyone else listens. It is a simple ritual, giving time for each individual in the group to share a concern, a feeling or some news. Where someone is non-verbal or has a more passive understanding of language, a helper might offer a 'doubling' statement for them. What is said must be done in a spirit of an offer, that is congruent to the mood of the participant, and the group leader should check with the group member that they agree with what is said. E.g., the helper might say, "I'm Dev, and I had a really difficult time getting up this morning, but I'm here now!" and the leader will ask "Is that so Dev?", inviting a nod or a gesture of dismissal. The appropriateness of using doubling in this way depends very much on the sensitivity of the helper. The principle is one of facilitating communication of a real felt sense, not creating an artificial version of the person being doubled. The technique of doubling comes from psychodrama psychotherapy and relies on a deep level of attunement and empathy.

## Purpose

This ritual gives form to the natural desire of people to share their news when they come together. It is often unrealistic to expect group members to participate in a session structure without the chance to get something off their chest first and to know that their individual voice has a place in the session. In the news round, everyone is heard, and everyone has a time to speak. Participants get to practise their communication and listening skills in a group context. The group leader may notice specific themes during the news round and incorporate these into the development of the session.

# News interview

## Preparation

An object that can represent a microphone is required. For suggestions, see 'News Round', above.

## Activity

The group leader, holding the 'microphone', stands in the middle of the circle and introduces herself as a well-known TV interviewer, such as Oprah Winfrey, or other current and local talk-show host, and welcomes the group to the show. She then introduces her first guest, one of the group members, and asks them a series of questions. Each group member will be interviewed in turn. The interviewer holds the microphone alternately to herself and to the interviewee. The following is a sample interview:

GROUP LEADER: So, ladies and gentleman, it's a great pleasure to welcome Edward Smith. A big hand, please, for Edward.

EDWARD: Thanks.

GROUP LEADER: Edward, tell me, what have you been doing this week? Working at all?

EDWARD: Yes, I work every day.

GROUP LEADER: Doing?

EDWARD: Washing the walls.

GROUP LEADER: Washing the walls. That sounds intriguing. Why have you been washing the walls?

EDWARD: We're painting the day centre. Got a party there soon. Maya's birthday. . .

- The key for the interviewer is to ask questions that are manageable and that will help the interviewee to remember what they have been doing and to value their own experience as news worth sharing. The less verbal members may be able to communicate quite a lot more with single words, sounds and nods in response to these questions than if left entirely to their own initiative to share some personal news.

# News interview

## Purpose

The small element of make-believe and role-play modelled by the group leader in this structure helps to prepare the group for later work in the session, while giving the opportunity for personal sharing. The mobile interviewer in the centre gives a clear focus for concentration, which can be particularly useful if group members find it difficult to listen to their peers.

## Further development

1 At the end of each interview ask the group/audience whose turn is next. Group members can volunteer or be chosen by their peers.

2 While interviewing, invite questions from the audience. For example:

> GROUP LEADER: Maya's party! That sounds interesting. Anyone have any questions for Edward about that?

> The microphone remains in the hands of the interviewer, and allows her to direct the group's attention.

3 Invite group members to take on the role of interviewer once they are familiar with what is expected. It takes quite some skill to keep a conversation going, and to react to what the interviewee has said, so they might like to start by interviewing the group leader, or someone else with good communication skills.

4 The interview technique can also be applied towards the end of a session as a preparation for closure (see *Chapter 12,* on de-roling).

# Introducing a neighbour

## Activity

Instead of each person introducing themselves to the group, the task here is for them to introduce a person sitting next to them to the group. The group leader can model this, so that the group has a basic pattern to follow. Start with a gesture and the neighbour's name, and follow with one piece of information about that person. For example:

GROUP MEMBER: This is Fran. Something I can tell you about Fran is . . . she's wearing new shoes today/she has a wonderful laugh.

## Purpose

This exercise requires participants to focus their interest and observation skills on another group member. Introducing a friend or colleague to a third party is also a useful social skill that is practised in this exercise. It is more challenging than introducing oneself, as the introducer has to take the feelings of their neighbour into account when sharing a piece of information about them.

## Further development

1 Over a period of sessions, encourage each group member to introduce someone different to the group and take a moment to check with that person "Is that right?"

2 Use the exercise to work on appropriate gesture, volume and pace of talking, as necessary. Ask the introducer to repeat the introduction, concentrating on one change. Group members can be encouraged to give each other supportive feedback.

CREATIVE DRAMA GROUPWORK FOR PEOPLE WITH LEARNING DIFFICULTIES

# Bongo conversation

## Preparation

A pair of bongos is required, with or without a stand.

## Activity

This exercise is often used in the context of music therapy, but it fits well into creative drama work. The bongos are placed between two group members, who turn to face each other. They have a 'conversation' together, by each beating, tapping, stroking or scratching the drum. If possible, they should find their own way of finishing, before passing the bongos on to another pair. The form of the bongo, which comprises two small drums joined together, allows each person to play on one half of the bongo, or to 'trespass' over to the other half, which can be quite dramatic.

## Purpose

This activity puts the non-verbal participants on an equal footing with the verbal members of the group. Each pair has the chance to express something unique together, and to be heard by the group as a whole. The playing may be tentative, gentle, playful, provocative, competitive, humorous or serious. The group listens to the different quality of each conversation.

## Further development

1 Ask the pair or the group as a whole for a title or a description of each conversation.

2 Notice how habitual communication patterns may be changed in this exercise. Someone who finds it hard to be assertive in general may be encouraged to use this exercise to make sure they get heard. Someone else who tends to dominate may be encouraged to listen and allow space for the other in the bongo conversation.

# Group shout

## Activity

Everyone holds hands to emphasize the connectedness of the group and takes a deep breath in preparation for a loud shout of "Hello!" The group leader counts down from three to one, and as the shout is delivered all hands reach upwards. If possible, use the energy of the shout and the joined hands to come from sitting to a standing position. Repeat the exercise a couple of times to find full energy and volume.

## Purpose

This exercise raises and focuses group energy. It can be particularly useful as a way of getting participants out of their seats and ready for more physical action. The anonymity of a group shout can help those group members who are shy or vocally inhibited to experience something of their vocal potential. In a world where people are often asked to 'behave' there is something joyful about having permission to make a noise together, however briefly.

## Further development

1 The silent shout. Try the whole exercise in silence, including opening the mouth and raising the arms as if shouting together. Use this as a build-up. Then do it with sound. It is like watching television with the sound down and then turning it up (see *Chapter 4* on voice work).

2 Initiate a specific kind of shout – e.g. a happy or celebratory shout of 'Yee hah!'

# 2

# Body
# Work

Awareness of the body is the first stage in
mindfulness. All the exercises in this section can
contribute to a mindful presence in the group.

# Warm-up yawn

## Activity

The yawn is a wonderful exercise to engage the whole body, breath and voice. Start small, with the mouth and jaw, then allow arms, sides of the torso and the whole body to join in, from face to feet. It is natural to include the voice, and this often occurs spontaneously. Yawning is contagious in a group and it is fun to have permission to really go for it collectively.

## Purpose

The group yawn is an energy raiser and a good way to start a physical warm up.

## Further development

1  In pairs, group members face each other and have a yawning conversation. Each yawn is answered by another yawn. Include the voice. Find a natural end to the conversation.

2  Choral yawning. Divide the group into two sub-groups, facing each other. Build an improvised conversation in yawns between one sub-group and the other.

BODY WORK 2

# Body parts

## Activity

With the group in a circle, the group leader demonstrates and talks through a number of physical movements focusing on each part of the body in turn. Each movement is repeated several times. Group members join in, to the best of their ability, all together.

- *Hands:* Open and close the fingers; shake the hands at the wrists to loosen, rotate at the wrists.

- *Elbows:* Bend the arms and make circles with the elbows, in both directions, large circles first, then small ones.

- *Shoulders:* With the arms by the sides, rotate both shoulder joints backwards and forwards; both shoulders together, then one at a time.

- *Arms:* Stretch the arms above the head and make circling and spiralling movements in all directions, bending the elbows as necessary.

- *Head and neck:* Slowly and gently lower the head forwards, while keeping the back straight. Bring the head up to a balanced starting position. From this position, turn the head to the right and to the left, without moving the shoulders and upper body.

- *Spine:* Make the spine as long as possible by feeling for an upwards pull through the top of the head and a downwards pull at the tail. Reach down towards the floor with arms and upper body; bend the knees a little and return to an upright position by uncurling the spine from the tailbone upwards: the last part to return to the upright is the head.

- *Pelvis:* Move the hips to the right and to the left by bending one knee at a time. Put the hands on the hips and make a big circle with the pelvis, parallel to the floor; first one way, then the other. Try making a figure of eight with the pelvis.

- *Knees:* Stand with the feet together, knees slightly bent. Put the hands on the knees and rotate; first one way then the other.

- *Legs:* Stand on one leg and let the other swing gently backwards and forwards at the hip; repeat with the other leg. Stand with legs wide apart and bend at one knee, taking the weight mostly onto that leg; keeping the

BODY WORK 2

# Body parts

body straight and arms relaxed, straighten that knee while bending the other: the weight is transferred to the other leg.

- *Feet:* Stand on one leg and rotate the free ankle in both directions; repeat with the other side. Lift one heel from the floor while keeping the toe on the ground; repeat, alternating the feet. Stand on tiptoe with both feet, and bring the heels down gradually. Shake out the whole body loosely like a rag doll.

## Purpose

The sequence helps to bring awareness to different parts of the body, and to develop confidence and balance. It is a good preliminary to free dance movement work. It is important to be aware of each person's level of physical ability, and the degree of effort, stretch and challenge involved for different individuals in the group.

## Further development

1 Each person in turn is asked to repeat their favourite movement and to lead the group in doing it together.

2 Use music to energize or give rhythm to the exercise.

# Hand massage

## Preparation

This is an exercise for pairs. Group members choose a partner they are happy to touch and be touched by. They sit together comfortably and close enough to be in easy reach of each other without stretching.

## Activity

Before making contact with his partner's hands, A, the masseur, rubs his own hands together briskly, to bring attention, awareness and warmth to them. He then takes one of *B's* hands between both his own and lets it rest there, with a firm, relaxed contact. Supporting *B's* hand from underneath with one hand, *A* strokes it repeatedly from just above the wrist down to the ends of the fingers, and beyond, as if stroking away any tension that has gathered there. In doing this *A* moves at a slow, relaxed pace, and concentrates just on his movements and his partner. He strokes again from just above the wrist, this time letting his hand slide towards his partner's thumb, and squeezes it gently, before letting it go, then repeating the movement, with the next and each subsequent finger, ending with the little finger. To end with *A* lets *B's* hand rest between both his hands again. The sequence is repeated with the other hand. *B* then performs the massage for *A*.

## Purpose

The exercise builds self-awareness and awareness of others. It requires and promotes trust. It brings up the question of appropriate and sensitive touch and mindful awareness to hands and the soothing quality of contact.

## Further development

1 Once the sequence is familiar, add relaxing, meditative music.

2 For an added sensory dimension, each pair is given scented hand cream, or a saucer of massage oil.

# Standing massage

## Preparation

This is an exercise for pairs. Group members choose a partner they are comfortable to touch and be touched by.

## Activity

The group leader demonstrates and describes the exercise first with a volunteer before talking the pairs through it. One partner, *A*, stands behind the other, *B*, who stands as comfortably as possible, with the weight evenly distributed between both feet. The active partner is told to proceed as follows. Place both hands on *B*'s shoulders and let them rest there for a moment. Then begin to circle and squeeze *B*'s shoulder area at a slow and steady rhythm. Now work down the back with downward strokes and circular movements, using the whole palm and fingers until the whole back has been contacted. Return to the base of the neck and gradually work down the spine, making little circles with two fingers on either side of the spine. Return to the shoulders and brush down the outer sides of the arms; then brush down the entire length of the back. Circle the area at the base of the spine a couple of times with the fingers; then, mobility allowing, slowly but firmly move the flat of both hands over the hip and buttock area and down the entire length of the legs to the ankles. In order to do this *A* needs to kneel down. From this position she holds the partner's ankles from behind and presses the heel firmly down towards the floor as if planting *B* in the ground. She remains in contact with *B's* feet for a while; this helps *B* to bring her attention down to the feet and to feel grounded.

## Purpose

The sequence promotes awareness of the full length of the body in both partners. It raises the issue of appropriate and sensitive touch, and can help to develop trust.

# Circle stretch

## Activity

The group stands in a circle and holds hands throughout the stretch. Together everyone stretches their arms towards the centre of the circle, to about shoulder height, then they lower the arms gradually to their sides. This is repeated at least once, as are all subsequent movements.

The hands are then taken backwards and stretched behind the circle, a movement which opens the chest area. Again they are returned to the sides.

Still holding hands, everyone now bends at the elbow, raises the arms and stretches straight up towards the ceiling. This elongating stretch should include the back, and a sense of the top of the head reaching upwards while the feet reach downwards.

The focus now moves to the legs. The held hands are used for mutual balance, or place the hands on the shoulders of your neighbours. With group members standing on one leg, the other leg is stretched towards the centre of the circle, a little way at first, then higher and as fully as possible. They repeat with the other leg.

Holding hands firmly for balance and standing on one leg, they stretch the other leg backwards as far as possible. (It helps to lean forward with the body.) They repeat with the other leg.

## Purpose

The sequence can be used as an energizing warm-up. There is a sense of group support and solidarity in being physically connected, and this can also help with concentration.

## Further development

Instead of each movement taking place in unison, one person starts a particular stretch, and the person standing next to them in the circle joins in as soon as they see and feel the movement. This sends a wave of movement around the circle.

# Scribble dance

## Preparation

Everyone needs a large piece of paper and either a coloured felt pen, wax crayon or pastel stick. Each person takes a place on the floor (or at a table if this is necessary) at a good arm's length from other group members with the paper in front of them.

## Activity

For the first part, writing implements and paper are left on the floor or table. Everyone is invited to close their eyes and to move their arms freely in all directions, 'scribbling' in the air. It may help to use an image: move the arms like two snakes, or like long grass in a stormy wind. Once the arms are loosened and moving freely, everyone opens their eyes, picks up their pen and locates their sheet of paper; then they close up their eyes again and scribble at random on their paper. There is no right or wrong in this – however it turns out is fine. On the instruction "Stop!" or "Freeze!" the pens are laid down and each person can see what kind of image they have created, and look at the various creations of the other group members.

For some groups the exercise may be considered complete at this stage. For those going on, the next stage involves interpreting each other's scribbles in dance, and can be done in pairs or groups of three. Partners or small groups choose each other in terms of whose scribble interests them. They spend some time looking at the scribble: how the line journeys across the page, how much space it uses, and the shapes, atmosphere and energy that it expresses. The scribbler then watches as the partner moves in the way they are inspired by the scribble. In this way each person has the opportunity to be choreographer, audience and dancer. The facilitator or helpers may model the whole process first.

## Purpose

Physically, the first part of the sequence helps to loosen the upper body and arms in particular, while the second part engages the whole body in creative movement. The sequence as a whole helps to build confidence in movement, personal expression and interpretation.

# Scribble dance

*continued from previous page*

## Further development

1 Pairs may be invited to show one or both of their scribble pictures and dances to the rest of the group.

2 The group as a whole may work together on one scribble picture and to memorize a whole sequence of movement, which could remain as an internal achievement of the group or be used as a performance project.

3 Work in a similar way to choreograph a dance based on a known piece of abstract art with plenty of movement in it, for example a painting by Joan Miró or Wassily Kandinsky.

4 Find words to describe some of the movements you have seen or done, e.g., up, down, round, spiky, dotty, wavy, twist, etc.

# Warm up exercise: Prune banana

## Preparation

No props are needed for this exercise, which usually creates a lot of laughter as well as warming up the voice and body. Be prepared to model the exercise with enthusiasm. This exercise could equally be included in the chapter on voice work.

## Activity

The group comes into a circle, large enough for everyone to stretch their arms without colliding with anyone.

Ask the group to repeat after you the word 'prune' and extend the word to 'prooooooon'. Describe the fruit, a dried-up plum that is shrivelled and wrinkly and compact. Now move the whole body and face to become as shrivelled and wrinkly and compact as a prune, whilst using the voice to illustrate the movement with the word 'prune'. For those able to, the movement includes squatting down, arms drawn in, face drawn in . . . not a pretty look! Come back to standing, and then ask the group to repeat the word 'banana'. Banana is the opposite of prune, bright, smiling and open. 'Bananaaa'. The movement to accompany this word is upwards and outwards, with wide eyes, wide arms, wide mouth, everything as wide and expanded as it can be.

Finally, put the two movements together in chorus. 'Prune, banana, prune, banana, prune, banana', each time committing more energy to getting the essence of these fruits and postures.

## Purpose

This is an energiser, activating a personal physical and vocal warm-up. At the same time it connects the group through a choral synchronized activity, and is nicely ridiculous.

## Further development

If you are inspired by other fruits, both in terms of their quality and the sound of their name, create your own movement and voice sequence. Develop a fruit salad!

# Trust exercise: Lying

## Preparation

Everyone finds a partner they are happy to work closely with and be touched by.

## Activity

The *As* lie down on their backs on a mat, preferably with eyes closed, and the group leader talks the *Bs* through some ways to help their partner become aware of their body and to relax.

*B* starts by holding her partner's feet, one hand on each foot. This position is maintained for a while so that *A* gets a chance to feel the contact and warmth of *B's* hands and to put his attention in his own feet.

*B* moves up to the side of *A's* body, and gently lifts one of his hands off the mat. A is encouraged to let his arm rest heavy in *B's* hands, and *B* may make small movements to encourage the arm to let go.

*B* moves around to the other side of *A's* body, where she can sit comfortably and repeat the procedure with the other hand.

*B* then moves up to behind *A's* head and places her hand on *A's* shoulders, helping them to open out and ease towards the mat.

*B* slides her hands under *A's* neck, and clasps the fingers of each hand together; then gently slides the hands upwards until they rest on the mat under *A's* head, which in turn rests in *B's* hands. *B* may rock the head very carefully and slowly to encourage her partner to release his neck muscles.

*B* comes round to the side of *A's* body again, places one hand to the side of *A's* hip, the other to the side of the ribs and gently pushes, so that his body rocks slightly and falls back towards *B's* hands. This rocking movement is repeated a few times, then *B* withdraws her hands and sits quietly at *A's* side for a few moments, before *A* is asked to open his eyes and gradually sit up.

The exercise is repeated with *B* on the mat and *A* helping.

# Trust exercise: Lying

## Purpose

The sequence helps participants develop a sense of their own body and how to relax. The physical contact can help in developing confidence and a sense of appropriate and sensitive touch.

## Further development

After the exercise, invite the whole group to lie down and to move their arms and legs freely to relaxing, flowing music, like seaweed moving under the water.

# Trust exercise: Sitting

### Preparation

The group splits into pairs of a similar size. Partners should be prepared to have physical contact together.

### Activity

Each pair sits back-to-back on a mat or on the floor. They think of their partner's back as the back of a comfortable chair, that they can sink into and that will give support. The group leader can go around and check each pair, to encourage a situation where each partner is leaning, rather than one where one person leans and the other supports. The goal is mutual trust, support and relaxation. Encourage each pair to take an in-breath together, and to let go a little more on the out-breath, which may be released as a relaxed sigh.

### Purpose

The exercise encourages a sense of mutual support. It helps participants become aware of tension and relaxation. The back-to-back position is less threatening than face-to-face, although for some participants any physical contact may be difficult.

### Further development

1 Introduce some gentle music and invite the pairs to allow their bodies to respond to the music while maintaining back-to-back contact.

2 In a group with verbal skills, invite the pairs to talk to each other while in a back-to-back position; they let each other know how they are feeling, how their week has been, and so on. The physical contact without eye contact provides an unusual and quite intimate basis for verbal sharing.

# Trust exercise: Standing

## Preparation

Everyone chooses a partner they are comfortable to work with closely, preferably of a similar height and weight.

## Activity

The group leader talks the pairs through various stages. First they stand back-to-back and let the two backs get to know each other, by wriggling up and down.

Then they stand still and let the two backs lean against each other peacefully, making sure that each person is being supported by their partner. It should be possible to feel themselves and their partner breathing.

## Purpose

The exercise brings awareness to the back as a part of the body, to the process of breathing and to the sense of relaxation, trust and letting go. It provides a foundation for the more challenging development, described below.

## Further development

Come together as a whole group. Each person is invited to be supported by the whole group. One at a time, they stand with both feet firmly on the floor and lean back, just a little way, while the rest of the group gives support with their hands. The group as a whole takes the weight of the individual who leans. The group leader makes sure that the responsibility for safety in this exercise is taken seriously by the group, and that the person who leans knows that it is not a matter of how far you lean, but a question of letting go as much as you are able to. It is not a question of free falling through the air: the group has contact with the individual's back throughout, and yields gently as the individual leans, while maintaining support. Touch is confined to areas of the body that are appropriate, mostly back, shoulders, arms, head.

# Trust exercise: Lifting

## Preparation

A large strong cloth is needed. The exercise is only possible with a group large enough and strong enough to support each person's weight fully and safely.

## Activity

The exercise is described first. Each person will have the opportunity to be lifted and carried by the group, who will try to make the experience a gentle and pleasant one. One person lies centrally on the cloth on the floor or mat. The group gather around, sitting on the floor, evenly spaced round the person lying down, so that, when it comes to lifting him, his weight is shared by the whole group. For the first couple of minutes they rest a hand gently on the part of the body closest to them. The person lying is encouraged to close their eyes, to feel the gentle contact of the group around them, and not to forget to breathe! Gradually, everyone moves their hands to grip the cloth firmly and stands up. The cloth is raised firmly and slowly a little way from the floor and the person lying in it has the experience of being lifted. One person takes responsibility for protecting the lying person's head, which may need a little extra support from underneath, and which should be the last part of the body to touch the ground when coming to land. The length of time each individual is carried in the cloth will depend on their level of comfort and relaxation, and the ability of the group to support them. If possible, make small rocking movements with the cloth, like very gentle waves on a shore; then take the individual for a slow journey around the room before coming to stillness and lowering them as gradually as possible back to the floor. The whole journey can be accompanied by a soothing humming of the group, or some pre-recorded relaxation music.

## Purpose

The experience for the individual can be one of a deep letting go, with a high degree of trust and enjoyment. At a group level, the process of looking after and the knowledge that the group can take care of each person in their vulnerability creates a strong bond.

# Trust exercise: Lifting

## Further development

Prepare the room with soft, coloured lighting and suitable music. As each person is lifted, talk them through an imaginary journey, such as a journey by boat on a starlit sea, where the group makes the sounds of the lapping waves, or of the music of the stars.

# Circle dance: Structured

## Preparation

The group leader chooses a piece of recorded music and spends some time familiarizing herself with it and trying out some possible moves. Suitable music can come from a wide variety of sources. Classical pieces such as Pachelbel's *Canon* can work well, as can folk music from different parts of the world such as Greece, South America or Ireland.

## Activity

Everyone holds hands in a circle and begins to move as directed by the group leader when the music plays. At the simplest level, the dance may consist of circling one way for a certain number of beats, and then in the other direction. Another simple structure is for everyone to move in together towards the centre of the circle and out again. A little more complicated is breaking into pairs and dancing with a partner for a set number of beats. Give plenty of time to return to the circle ready for the next phrase of music.

A more demanding variation is for the circle to break at one point and for two end people to make an arch. The person at the other end leads the group through the arch and back into a circle. The key for the group leader is to make the structure simple enough for the group to achieve it, with enough challenge to keep it interesting. Talk the group clearly through the dance as each new phrase comes up. The music may suggest particular variations, such as a moment to clap hands, stamp feet or reach up with the arms.

## Purpose

The circle dance can create a sense of unity and harmony in a group. It requires a certain amount of concentration, but is containing and relatively undemanding. You can use it as a closure at the end of a session as well as a warm-up at the beginning (see *Chapter 13*, on closures).

# Circle dance: Structured

## Further development

1 Repeat and develop the dance over a number of sessions, including new elements each time. Take suggestions from the group for particular phrases, or to determine the sequence of phrases.

2 Create a dance around a particular theme. Cyclical themes such as the harvest or New Year are particularly appropriate.

BODY WORK 2

# Circle dance: Free

### Preparation

The group leader chooses some recorded music. Music with a strong beat can help inspire movement. Some hand-held percussion instruments give an added expressive dimension. They can be left close at hand until needed.

### Activity

The group forms a circle and moves to the music. Movement suggestions are made non-verbally, and the group leader can model being aware of and following the movements made by other group members. In this way a fluid dance-movement improvisation can take place that is unique to a particular group at a particular moment. At some point the invitation is given for someone to enter the centre of the circle and dance there in their own way. The rest of the group continues moving to the music and supports the individual in the centre by clapping to the beat, or playing a small percussion instrument. When they are ready (or when prompted) they rejoin the circle and someone else goes into the middle.

### Purpose

This dance promotes spontaneity and an awareness of the group as a whole and individuals in it. As long as the circle is maintained there is no right or wrong, and each person's contribution is valued. This helps promote confidence and is fun.

### Further development

Give individuals a chance to invite a partner into the circle, so that there are two people finding their way of dancing together within the circle.

BODY WORK
2

# Elastic dance

## Preparation

A piece of strong elastic, at least 5 cm (2 inches) wide, and long enough to encircle the drama group (3 to 6 metres – 10 to 20 feet) is sewn into a circle. This forms the basis for the elastic circle dance, and is also a useful general prop for use in improvisation work. Recorded or streamed music is optional.

## Activity

The group stands in a circle, each person holding on to the elastic. The dance comprises a sequence of movements that can be prepared in advance by the group leader or which can arise spontaneously in the group. The elastic literally ensures that the group members stay connected with each other. Possibilities include the following:

- Everyone moves backwards together, stretching the elastic circle as far as possible, then they move in towards the centre again.

- Some participants on one side of the circle keep their place while others move towards them, eventually bouncing off the elastic and returning to their side of the circle. The wave of movement is random and energetic.

- Everyone together lifts the elastic high into the air and brings it down behind their backs to waist level. They try leaning back and letting the elastic give support. If possible, they release their hold.

- The group eases the elastic down their backs, and towards the floor; then lifts it again in front of the body.

## Purpose

The use of the elastic is particularly suitable for people who do not like to hold hands or who need more space. It helps a group maintain a circle and a sense of connection. It is a useful device for exploring issues of distance, connection and proximity.

## Further development

One person at a time has the chance to move individually in and out, over or under the elastic, making their own individual dance, while the group as a whole maintains the circle.

# Hoop dance

## Preparation

One hula hoop is needed per person. A variety of colours gives added visual interest. Have some recorded or streamed music ready to play. Give some time for free exploration, for getting to know what is possible with a hula hoop. Participants can try holding, dropping, rolling and spinning the hoop on the floor, swirling it around their bodies and rolling or throwing the hoop to a partner. At the end of the exploratory time, each person or pair may like to show the group one possibility they have discovered.

## Activity

Each person holds on to their own hoop with one hand and on to another person's with the other, so that a large circle is created. As the music begins to play, a variety of visual effects can be created by dancing with the hoops. Possibilities include the following:

- Stand still with arms out to the sides. Rotate the wrists and see the hoops turn.

- Move arms in large backward circles from the shoulders.

- Raise and lower each arm alternately to create a wave effect.

- Crouch or bend towards the floor, and shake the hoops to create a rattling noise against the floor.

- The circle rotates in each direction, by pacing, skipping or running as the music suggests.

- One person lets go with one hand, so that the circle becomes a chain. The leader takes the group on a journey around the room, eventually joining up to create the circle again.

## Purpose

The hoops give an incentive for movement. For some people it is more interesting to relate to a prop than to move for its own sake. The hoops are light and easy to lift and give a satisfying aesthetic result.

# Hoop dance

### Further development

1 Maintaining the circle, each person lets go one hand so that everyone is holding just their own hoop again. They lift the hoop up, pass it over their head and bring it down to the floor, so that they are standing inside it. From this position group members can wave to someone across the circle and, if the wave is returned, move across the circle and swap places.

2 Musical hoops. All hoops are on the ground. As the music plays everyone dances freely outside the hoops. When it stops they have to find their way into a hoop as fast as possible. There is no penalty for being last but, each time the sequence is repeated, the group leader takes away one hoop, so that more and more people have to share. The final challenge is for everyone to get some part of their body into the final hoop. (See *Chapter 6*, on games.)

**BODY WORK 2**

# Cloth dance

### Preparation

A selection of cloths is required, varying in size, colour and texture; also some recorded, streamed or live music.

### Activity

Everyone chooses a cloth that appeals to them or that suits their mood. As the music plays, they begin to move or dance with the cloth. Each person may dance for themselves or make contact with other people in the dance.

### Purpose

The cloths help to inspire movement and contact, and the result is aesthetically rewarding.

### Further development

Everyone holds on to their own cloth and that of one other person. The group creates a tangle. When the tangle is at its worst, they try to reverse the process while keeping hold of the cloths.

BODY WORK 2

# Fan dance

## Preparation

Each person needs a decorative fan. (These can be bought or made by the group as a preliminary project.) For full effect, the fans do need to be quite stiff. Some dignified recorded music is also required, such as a classical minuet or waltz. Dressing up clothes or cloths to drape help with entering the spirit of the dance.

## Activity

The group leader introduces the idea that the group is invited to a stately ball, for which they may like to dress up. Having chosen their pieces of costume, everyone finds a partner with whom they would like to dance. They enter the space designated as the ballroom, and may be announced respectfully by the group leader as doorkeeper with suitable aristocratic titles. Before the music plays, remind everyone that the idea of the dance is to keep eye contact with the partner and to let the two fans dance with each other. As the music begins and ends they may bow or curtsey, and this can be practised as a group before starting the music. Once the first dance is over, they may like to change dancing partners for the next one. At the end of the ball, allow the group time to put away the costumes and fans, and to let go of the roles that they have played. Come back into the here and now with some discussion of what each person enjoyed best or did not like.

## Purpose

This activity uses dance to enter into a guided role-play situation (see *Chapters 8* and *9*, on improvisation and dramatization). The fans may inspire a non-habitual way of dancing. They can provide some welcome distance from the partner, or act as a bridge through which to maintain contact. The noble roles adopted and the special situation of the ball allow people to explore a different style of being together for the duration of the role-play.

## Further development

1 Introduce a court photographer, perhaps the group leader within the role-play who asks the various couples to pose for the camera or takes

# Fan dance

• • • • • • • • • • • • • • • • • • • • • • • • • • • • • • • • • • • • • • • • • • • • • •

*continued from previous page*

a group photograph. If a real camera is used, the group can look at the photographs and compile a newspaper, radio report or blog of the ball in the following session.

2 The group develops further the characters introduced in the role-play and creates a story based on a selection of them.

CREATIVE DRAMA GROUPWORK FOR PEOPLE WITH LEARNING DIFFICULTIES

# Statues

## Preparation

This activity requires musical accompaniment, set up in such a way that it can be repeatedly stopped and started. The group is prepared for free movement with a guided physical warm-up (for example, 'Body Parts', above, p. 50).

## Activity

As the music plays, group members dance or move freely around the room. The moment the music stops, accompanied if necessary by the back-up instruction to "Freeze!", everyone holds their position like a statue, until the music begins again.

## Purpose

This structure encourages listening, free movement and an awareness of stopping and starting. Holding the statue positions gives a natural opportunity to work on balance within a variety of postures.

## Further development

1 Look at pictures of real statues of people and abstract shapes. Try to recreate them within the group using bodies and objects.

2 As a group, visit a museum, art gallery, stately home or public place with real statues. Look at their postures and what they express, and at their stillness and sense of movement. In the next session, create statues in pairs or small groups. Each person in turn is the sculptor. Their partners allow themselves to be physically moulded and verbally directed into shape. Each sub-group displays one of its creations to the rest of the group, announcing its title or letting the group as a whole decide on one.

3 Create expressive groupings of people as if posing for a photograph. On the instruction "Freeze!" everyone is still and the group leader takes a real or imaginary photograph.

4 Give a theme for the group to compose statues together, e.g. Spring, Friendship, Sadness, Conflict, Joy. Name the theme, and use a percussion instrument to indicate the moment to hold the image and to look around at what the group has created spontaneously.

**BODY WORK 2**

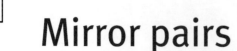

# Mirror pairs

## Preparation

Everyone chooses a partner they are happy to move with. Set up some pre-recorded music: something light, flowing and slow works well.

## Activity

Partners stand opposite each other with enough space for them to be able to touch if they both stretch forward. One person is a mirror, and whenever their partner moves a part of their body, they reflect the movement immediately. Before starting the music it is worth clarifying with a short practice run which arm and which leg are opposite which. Partners must remain focused on each other throughout, either with eye contact or with a more general gaze at the whole body. Movements should be very slow and simple. The group leader may need to give each pair some individual attention, reminding them to stay focused on each other, or to move more slowly. After practising for a while with the music, each partner being in role as mirror and as mover, invite any pairs who wish to perform their work for the group to do so.

## Purpose

The exercise can create a strong non-verbal rapport between the partners. It requires sensitivity and concentration. As an exercise in body awareness and focus it promotes mindfulness.

## Further development

1 Each pair finds another pair and they form a circle. One person leads, and the others mirror the movements. Participants take it in turns to lead.

2 In pairs, group members sit opposite each other on chairs and focus on the face. One person leads by making slowly changing facial expressions and the other mirrors as accurately as possible.

3 Introduce a real full-length or hand-held mirror to the group. Just look, or use it as a chance to explore self-image, by discussing what each person sees.

4 Explore face painting and make-up in the group, using real mirrors. Repeat the original mirror pair exercise with painted faces and an item of costume. The element of disguise may inspire new ways of moving.

BODY WORK 2

# Bird pairs

## Preparation

The group splits into pairs or groups of three. In each pair, one plays the role of the parent bird, the other the egg. In a group of three there will be two eggs. The group leader gives an outline for the movement improvisation that will follow. All the parent birds will build a nest out of cloths and cushions where they can sit with their egg. When the young bird inside the egg is ready, it taps on its shell and finds its way out into the world. It discovers its body and its parent. The parent bird must feed it and keep it safe. After a while it must teach it to fly. Once the young bird leaves the nest, it is possible that it will meet other birds or baby birds. The whole piece is accompanied by evocative music, such as music of flute or pan pipes, something that is airy and flowing. Make sure there are plenty of cloths, cushions and rugs to build nests.

## Activity

The movement improvisation will have its own pace and rhythm. It starts very still and peaceful, and gradually becomes more energetic and playful. If the group needs prompting, the group leader may accompany the improvisation with an occasional narrative, allowing plenty of time for each phase. Bring the improvisation to a close at the end of an imaginary day, with everyone resting.

After clearing away props, create a circle. Ask all those who played parent birds and all those who played baby birds to describe what it was like, what they did and how it felt (see *Chapters 8* and *12*, on improvisation and de-roling). This feedback may be done in a physical way by reprising a key moment from the exercise sequence.

## Purpose

The piece allows free movement within given guidelines and supported by a musical accompaniment. The imaginary context gives the opportunity to explore themes of closeness, dependence and independence, caring and risk-taking.

# Bird pairs

*continued from previous page*

## Further development

1 Discuss how it feels to learn something for the first time and to take a risk. What moments have group members known that have felt like learning to fly?

2 Discuss how it feels to help or look after someone. What experiences have group members had in their own lives of helping or looking after someone?

# 3

# Sensory Work

Being in touch with senses brings us into the here and now. All the exercises in this section can contribute to a mindful presence in the group.

# Autumn leaf experience

## Preparation

Gather a sack or two of dry autumn leaves.

## Activity

Pass the closed sack around and ask the group to guess what it might be, by experiencing its weight and the sounds it makes. Empty the leaves in a large heap on the floor. (If mess is a problem, lay down a large sheet.) Invite the group to get to know the leaves in different ways; to touch the leaves with their hands; to scrunch them with their fingers; to lift a few leaves up as high as possible and let them fall to the ground; to lie down and roll in the leaves; to sit in them and whoosh them around with hands and legs; to stand up and march through them.

## Purpose

A feast for all the senses, an opportunity to play, regardless of age.

## Further development

After the group has experienced the leaves for themselves, they can encounter them again from within a dramatic role. Tell the following (or a similar) story which the group illustrates in movement, incorporating the real leaves. Roles can be allocated, or everyone can play all the roles, moving from one to the other as the story progresses.

There was once a young squirrel that was born in the spring when the leaves were green. It lived all summer in the woods, and enjoyed sitting in the sun, running through the soft grass, climbing up the trees, looking for food, eating and sleeping. One morning it woke up and felt a single leaf falling on its nose. It looked up, surprised, and, sure enough, leaves were falling down from the sky as if it were raining leaves. The squirrel had never seen anything like it. It picked up a fallen leaf and looked at its golden colour. It held it between its paws and heard it crackle like fire. It listened to the wind blowing and watched as more and more leaves came falling out of the trees. This was fun, and the squirrel ran and skipped through the leaves, throwing them in the air, crunching them beneath its feet and shouting, "Autumn's

# Autumn leaf experience

*continued from previous page*

here, autumn's here!" It played in the leaves until it was quite tired and the sun was setting. Then it lay down in the leaves, made itself comfortable and went to sleep.

It is important to give space and structure for the group to leave the role of the squirrel, and come back to their own role. After lying for a while in the leaves, group members are asked to leave the sleeping squirrels, stand up as themselves and brush off any leaves. In brushing off the leaves they are also brushing off the remnants of the role and contacting their own familiar body. (See *Chapter 12*, on de-roling.)

# Journey through the elements

## Preparation

Set out the following items in various parts of the drama space: a large bowl of water and a jug (the water can be scented with a few drops of lemon juice or essential oil); a mound of fresh soil (perhaps surrounded by a circle of pebbles); a candle in a candle holder (perhaps one with a facility to hold an essential oil); a fan (hand-held or electric). Each zone can be further defined with coloured cloths, cushions and so on.

## Activity

Group members are escorted individually through the zones, and guided in so far as this is necessary, to explore with their escort the nature of each element. The many possibilities include the following:

- pouring water from jug to bowl,
- pouring water over hands,
- dipping hands in water,
- rubbing soil between hands,
- smelling soil,
- feeling pebbles,
- clinking pebbles together,
- watching the movement of the flame,
- hand dancing around the candle,
- holding hands close to the flame and feeling the warmth,
- exploring the movement of the fan,
- fanning the face,
- fanning wet hands.

The whole journey may be accompanied by slow, spacious and relaxing music.

# Journey through the elements

*continued from previous page*

## Purpose

Opening the senses, relaxation, developing trust in the environment and another person, a chance for non-verbal exploration.

## Further development

1 Those who have been guided through the journey take on the role of guide, and the guides become the guided. It is important for people with learning difficulties, who are often in the role of passive recipients, to have the opportunity to explore leadership and active giving. It is also useful for staff members and helpers to be open to readily accept a receiving role.

2 In a following session the group creates a sequence of mimes relating to the journey. Together these mimes tell the story of the journey through the elements. By repeating the movements, group members may also be able to evoke imaginatively the particular sensations of the previous session.

# Sounds from things

## Activity

The core idea is that everything can be a musical instrument within the context of a creative drama session. The group is encouraged to find ways of getting objects to 'sing'. A guided tour of the creative drama space reveals such 'instruments' as radiators, walls, table tops, cushions, doors and handles. These objects are an intrinsic part of the space. Further props of an everyday nature, such as pots and pans, boxes, baskets, bottles and jars, can be added to extend the repertoire.

Group members first explore different ways of using their hands to create sounds, such as tapping, knocking, rubbing, flicking and finger drumming on a variety of surfaces. The same objects can then be 'played' with musical beaters, or short sticks, exploring different rhythms and strengths of playing. In order to avoid a cacophony, the group leader can structure this experimental phase of the session by giving group members time to explore an object in turn, or in pairs. After a thorough exploration, everyone chooses one 'instrument' to play by hand or with the beaters. The group leader takes on the role of conductor, and practises the signals for 'start playing' and 'stop' with the whole group. She then conducts an improvised piece, giving each person a short solo, and conducting pairs or small groups to play while the rest listen and wait for their turn to be conducted in.

## Purpose

This exercise emphasizes the senses of hearing and touch, encouraging a playful spirit of investigation and exploration, while demanding active listening and concentration. This activity offers an opportunity for non-verbal exploration.

## Further development

1 Group members take it in turns to be the conductor. A special jacket, gloves and baton add authority to the role.

2 Half the group gives a performance of an improvised piece to the other half. They may like to give the work a title before playing it or afterwards. The sub-groups then reverse roles.

SENSORY WORK

# Sounds from things

*continued from previous page*

**3** The group makes instruments together in preparation for further improvisation. Jars of various sizes filled with dried beans or grains make interesting shakers.

A set of bottles can be tuned to a scale by adding varying degrees of water and tapping with a beater. Try blowing across the opening of other bottles. 'Rain sticks' can be made by filling plastic tubing with beads and sealing each end with a metal lid. When the rain stick is tipped slowly, the beads drop and create the sound of falling rain. These hand-made instruments can be used to create a unique musical band, or can be used to complement more traditional musical instruments.

SENSORY WORK

# Sounds in the wood

## Preparation

A bamboo garden cane about a metre (3 feet) long is needed for each person. The activity works best on a wooden or other non-carpeted floor.

## Activity

Everyone has a cane and explores it with the guidance of the group leader. It can be held in one hand or two, vertically or horizontally. It is hollow, and one end is broader than the other. By blowing across this end it may be possible to produce a whistling sound, like the wind blowing. Try also holding the stick in one hand vertically and passing it from one hand to the other with a steady rhythm. After some time has been allowed for each individual to get familiar with the feel of their cane and the way it moves, the focus moves on to a group level.

The group stands in a circle, each person holding their cane, with the thinner end on the floor. The canes are held at arm's length, extended towards a central point on the floor, where all canes meet. At first they are held still, then slowly all the tips are shaken gently to vibrate against each other and produce a quiet rustling. This develops into a gentle, slow tapping on the surface of the floor, which can get louder or softer, faster or slower at the direction of the group leader. The sound can be varied by striking other canes. For the sake of safety, remind the group to keep the ends of the canes close to the ground and to strike only the far end of the canes together.

For a more explosive sound, each person holds their cane high and parallel to the floor. At an agreed moment, everyone lets go of their canes and listens to the clatter as they fall. If space allows, everyone comes to one end of the floor with their canes and one or two at a time roll them along the floor as far as they can.

The sequence finishes in contrasting silence. The group comes back into a circle, cane points together at a central point of the floor. All together, they raise their canes slowly as high as they can go, creating a 'roof' over the centre of the circle. The roof is lowered, with contact and control being maintained, and the canes end up on the floor like the spokes of a wheel.

SENSORY WORK 3

# Sounds in the wood

*continued from previous page*

The whole sequence, having been practised, can be repeated and brought to life by using it to illustrate the following (or a similar) story. Decide with the group which movements with the canes best reproduce the desired sounds.

It seems like a quiet day in the forest, but there is a storm in the air. Occasionally, you can just hear the wind breathing and whistling amongst the trees, and there is a faint rustling among the leaves. Slowly but surely, the first raindrops begin falling onto the leaves and ground. There isn't much rain at first, just a gentle pattering; but then it begins to come down faster – small drops at first, then big, loud ones. It's really pelting down, and there might even be thunder: one sharp, deafening thunder clap, followed by more rolling thunder, loud at first then fading into the distance. All the creatures and people of the forest are finding shelter from the rain and the wind, waiting for the storm to pass. At last it's over and you can hear the silence, and smell the freshness in the air.

## Purpose

The sequence encourages listening and sensory imagination. The formal use of the sticks requires control, initially through the group leader's instructions, then perhaps increasingly in the form of self-discipline and self-confidence.

## Further development

In a subsequent session the group listens to the story again while lying or sitting relaxed. In this way the physical, sensory experience is used as a foundation for a guided fantasy.

# Parachute

## Preparation

A round, coloured parachute is ideal, especially for a group of eight or more. These can be bought through therapy and education equipment catalogues. Although expensive, they are a very popular and accessible prop. For a smaller group, or if funds do not run to a parachute, any large piece of material can be used, as long as it is not too heavy and can withstand a certain amount of strain.

## Activity

The group stands in a circle, each person holding the edge of the parachute. Everyone raises and lowers their arms together. The parachute looks impressive as it moves, catching the air underneath it. It also creates a wonderful breeze. Variations such as the following are explored:

- Everyone leans back, making the parachute taut, then raising and lowering it slowly, feeling the resistance of the air.

- The parachute is lifted as high as possible towards the ceiling, filling with air, and is taken down as low as possible towards the floor.

- The parachute is shaken up and down with short, fast movements.

- Some hold the parachute higher, others lower, and the parachute is moved up and down to create waves.

- The parachute is moved gently and smoothly, with a minimum of effort.

- A storm is created by holding it taut and moving it fast, loudly and with maximum effort.

- The parachute is held close to the floor and short waves are sent across it.

- The whole sequence can be accompanied by a piece of evocative music, something that includes both peaceful and stormy passages, and that calls to mind scenes from the countryside or the sea.

## Purpose

The parachute provides a rewarding collective experience. The demand on each individual is not great, but the overall effect is particularly rich at a

# Parachute

*continued from previous page*

sensory level. There is a strong sense of the body in movement, the touch of moving air on skin and hair. The activity also gives an experience of weight and lightness, and of colour in movement.

## Further development

1 Throw an inflated ball, such as a beach ball, onto the parachute. The group works together to send it flying into the air and rolling round the parachute without falling off.

2 The group raises the parachute as high up as possible, and group members make eye contact with each other underneath it. Two people at a time change places under the parachute while it is up in the air. It is best to work with a regular rhythm and to give the two people some notice before they cross; for example, "The *next* time it's up, Sara and Ahmed change places. . . ready. . . and. . ." For a final round that is fun, ask everyone to change places at the same time. The parachute is released at its highest point, and comes down at random, amid a general free-for-all and much laughter.

3 For a group with physical flexibility and confidence, the parachute can be transformed into a tent in which everyone sits. The parachute is lifted high, as normal, then everyone takes one step in towards the middle of the circle, brings the parachute down behind their heads, squats right down to the floor and ends up sitting inside the parachute with its edge tucked under their bottoms. Everyone leans back a little against the inside walls of the parachute/tent until it becomes taut. Once this is achieved, the group can begin a dramatic improvisation, deciding together where they might be, and what they might be doing there. For example, they could be in a tent in the desert or in a hot-air balloon flying over the mountains.

# Colour palette

## Preparation

A variety of cloths of different colours are needed, including a mixture of strong and pastel colours.

## Activity

The cloths are laid out where they can be touched and examined. Everyone chooses the colour that most attracts them at that moment. They can hold the cloth, sit or lie on it or drape themselves in it. Each person has the opportunity to say something about their choice, such as the name of the colour, an object that comes to mind in relation to the colour, or what mood the colour represents. A non-verbal alternative is for each person to show the group their cloth and how they can move with it.

The group then creates a work of art by arranging the cloths together. The group leader gives a framework for this, by defining an area of floor space as the canvas, or by making a three-dimensional structure using perhaps a chair and table. One by one, each group member comes into this space and places their cloth where they would like to see it, in relation to the space and in relation to the other colours. An abstract picture emerges, which the group can look at, give a title to, and photograph.

## Purpose

The exercise encourages an awareness of colour and gives the opportunity to express preferences and make aesthetic choices. There is no right and wrong in this exercise and it can give satisfaction to all ages and levels of ability.

## Further development

1 The colour collage can be used as a background for each person to place themselves individually in a chosen position somewhere in the space and to be photographed. The same can be done with pairs.

2 An alternative collage is created by one person draping himself in his chosen cloth, then taking up a position within the framed space. The others join in one by one, having looked at the collage and considered how and where to position themselves.

# Colour palette

*continued from previous page*

**3** After a session or more working with awareness of colour, group members are invited to close their eyes and allow a colour or selection of colours to come to mind. Each person 'paints' their image for the group, using the familiar cloths, and gives the picture a title.

# Streamers

## Preparation

Coloured streamers are needed, approximately 4 metres (12 feet) long and four centimetres (an inch and a half) wide. The best material is satin, which is smooth and has some weight. The streamers may be attached to a stick or held directly in the hand. Rhythmic, flowing recorded music accompanies the activity.

## Activity

Everyone holds a streamer and moves it freely to the music as they move around the room. Streamers may come into contact with each other, and may be used to make gentle or playful contact with other group members. Group members or group leader may also initiate more focused movement. By holding all the streamers so they touch the floor and wiggling them fast from side to side, the group can create the effect of colourful snakes on the ground. By lifting them high and making large swirling circles, they can make a cloudy sky in the wind. By whipping the streamers upwards briskly, they can make the effect of flames dancing in a fire.

## Purpose

The streamers magnify the effect of each movement. They stimulate the imagination and promote indirect physical contact.

## Further development

1 The group divides into pairs. Each pair holds one streamer between them and finds ways of moving with it. As pairs meet, they make new patterns with their streamers. Eventually, the whole group comes together. Streamers may cross and become tangled. The group then works together to become untangled.

2 The streamers can also be used when the group is sitting in a circle, to wind down at the end of a session. Each person is connected to two other people by holding one end of a streamer in each hand. A network of coloured streamers is woven between all group members as a symbol of the many contacts in the group (see *Chapter 13*, on closures).

# 4

# Voice Work

Voice connects our body with expression. There is a strong link between voice and the emotions. We carry our inhibitions and something of our self-image in our voice. We can all benefit from increasing our voice repertoire, something that is allowed and encouraged within a creative drama group.

# Loosening up

## Preparation

The group stands in a circle, large enough to stretch the arms wide without touching anyone.

## Activity

Standing upright with legs comfortably wide, feet slightly turned out and the arms loose at the side, group members turn the upper body to the side, first one way and then the other. The movement is loose, fluid and relaxed. The head and neck remain in line with the trunk. When turning towards the right, the left knee bends a little, and vice versa. If the arms are relaxed they will swing out away from the body a little and gently strike the torso as the direction changes. The movement is done in an easy rhythm for some minutes.

Make sure the face is relaxed, the mouth loose and a little open. Participants continue the movement while yawning and sighing nonchalantly, with an 'aah' sound. The mood is deliberately lazy, as if using a minimum of energy. The yawn encourages a deep relaxed inhalation, while the sigh ensures a full, easy exhalation. To keep the lips relaxed, they breathe out to a 'Whh' sound.

## Purpose

The exercise prepares the body, breath and face for voice work. It can be used as a relaxation exercise in its own right.

VOICE WORK

# Freeing the face

### Preparation

The group stands or sits with an open and upright posture in a circle. The group leader talks through the exercise before demonstrating it. (It is hard to describe it and do it at the same time.)

### Activity

Making chewing and stretching movements, try to exercise all the muscles of the face. Open the mouth, eyes and whole face as wide as possible. Close everything as small as possible. Move the face into a series of unlikely expressions. Surprise yourself.

Use the fingers to make circular kneading movements around the jaw, cheeks and forehead. Repeat the chewing and stretching movements. With the mouth closed, move the tongue around the mouth between the teeth and lips several times in each direction.

### Purpose

The face is often neglected as a part of the body to be exercised. It is particularly relevant to ensure it is relaxed and flexible when approaching voice work as it is a vital part of the vocal instrument.

### Further development

Go through the exercise again while vocalizing with whatever sounds accompany the movements. An unusual series of sounds will emerge.

**VOICE WORK 4**

# Letting go flop

## Preparation

The group stands in a circle. The group leader models the exercise. Group members watch first, then try it for themselves.

## Activity

Standing with legs comfortably wide, reach upwards with the arms, stretching right through to the fingertips and trying to be as tall as possible. Hold the stretch while breathing in. Use maximum effort, then on the instruction "Flop!" let the whole upper body flop forward towards the floor on the out-breath. Bend the knees at the same time and allow the arms to swing loosely. Pay attention to letting the neck relax and the head hang loosely. The moment of letting go is accompanied by a free groan or vocalized sigh with an open mouth. The relaxation of the body helps the voice to come out in an easy way.

Uncurl from the base of the spine upwards, leaving the neck and head until last. Repeat the exercise several times, trying to increase the initial effort and the subsequent floppiness with each attempt. The group leader may need to give some individual attention to help participants to master the uncurling movement. A hand placed gently on the lower back can help with locating the initial impulse. A hand resting lightly on the head and neck can serve as a reminder not to tense these muscles as the back uncurls.

## Purpose

By the relaxing and opening of the body and breath, the voice is freed. This exercise works with the natural connection between posture, musculature, breath and voice.

## Further development

Once the basic exercise is mastered, try using the tongue and mouth while flopping, to create loose nonsense sounds.

# Sound echo

## Preparation

This exercise is best attempted after some physical warm-ups, as described above. The group stands in a large circle. The sense of space is important to encourage volume and voice projection.

## Activity

The group is asked to listen carefully to the sounds the leader makes, to wait a moment, then to echo them back as a whole group. The group leader uses simple vowel sounds, and calls them with a relaxed open throat. The voice is used in an easy style between shouting and singing. It should feel relaxed, clear and able to carry well. Suggest the image of calling from one mountain to another, the group acting as an echo, as might happen in nature. Some good sounds to use are the following:

- Aah (as in 'far', with a long mouth)

- Eh (as in 'hay', with a wide mouth)

- Aw (as in 'four' with the lips forward)

- Eeh (as in 'see')

Pitch the sound on one extended note, or move rhythmically between two or three notes. The emphasis is on the quality of openness of the voice and the accuracy of listening and reproduction of the sound. As the group gets more proficient, combine different vowel sounds and notes.

## Purpose

This exercise works with listening and reproducing sound playfully without being dependent on words or tied to notions of singing. It can help instil confidence in using the voice, as the group makes the sounds loudly and in unison.

## Further development

1 The group leader calls to an individual in the group, who echoes the sound back alone. The sound can be repeated several times and the individual

VOICE WORK

4

# Sound echo

encouraged to repeat it more confidently each time, as he gets more used to hearing his own voice.

2 The role of caller is taken by other group members in turn, and the group echoes their sounds back to them as above.

# Sliding scale

## Activity

The group stands in a large circle. The exercise involves standing upright and comfortably with feet a little apart, arms loosely at the sides of the body. The arms are raised forwards and upwards, extremely slowly, over the course of several minutes, and then down again at a similar speed. The movement accompanies a vocal journey that begins on as low a note as the group can hold, and rises imperceptibly to as high a note as possible. The vowel sound used is 'aw' as in 'saw' for the low and middle notes, moving into 'oo' as in 'too' for the high notes. The movement of pitch is a gradual, sliding, *glissando* one. Each person breathes as necessary, while the group as a whole holds the tone, so that the sound is continuous. Try to maintain the quality of listening as a group so that each gradual movement of arms and tone happens in unison.

## Purpose

The physical movement helps to make the gradual vocal shifts visual and tangible. A high note is literally accompanied by reaching high; a low note by reaching low.

## Further development

The basic exercise benefits from practice over a period of time as a regular part of the creative drama session. Once there is a degree of mastery, try dividing into two sub-groups. Each sub-group holds a different note, or slides between a small range of notes. The two sub-groups practise individually at first, then try to hold their own notes while vocalizing at the same time.

CREATIVE DRAMA GROUPWORK FOR PEOPLE WITH LEARNING DIFFICULTIES

# Volume control

## Preparation

Each person chooses a sentence which they can use throughout the exercise. It may be something topical, such as 'Liverpool won the match last night'; a line from a well-known play, such as 'To be or not to be, that is the question' or 'If music be the food of love, play on!'; or a proverb, such as 'A stitch in time saves nine'.

## Activity

The sentence is used to practise speaking at different volumes. This may be done in pairs or as a whole group. Begin by coming in very close and whispering the sentence as if it were a secret not to be overheard. Move slightly apart and say the sentence quietly to a neighbour, as if talking privately with a friend. Move a little further apart and address the whole group, a little more loudly, as if talking to a group of friends and wanting them all to hear. Move as far apart as possible, and call the sentence as if trying to tell someone something very important across a crowded station.

## Purpose

Appropriate volume depends on distance and social context. This exercise gives an opportunity to play with this, and to practise using the voice in a variety of ways. The emphasis is less on what is being said and more on the way it is said.

## Further development

1 In pairs, demonstrate speaking at the wrong volume for the distance. The group gives feedback.

2 Using nonsense or gobbledygook phrases, pairs perform improvised conversations. The group guesses what kind of conversation they might be having just from the tone of voice; for example, an argument, a conspiracy or a proposal.

3 Those who are speaking a second language or are bilingual can teach the group a sentence or phrase from their own mother tongue.

VOICE WORK 4

# Throrwing the voice

## Preparation

A large ball is needed for this structure. An inflatable ball is best, large but not too heavy.

## Activity

The group stands in a large circle. The ball is thrown from one person to another across the circle. It is important that the distance demands some effort on the part of the thrower. The action accompanies a call of "Ahoy" and the name of the recipient. The recipient chooses the next person to throw to.

## Purpose

The trajectory of the ball is also the trajectory of the voice, and the physical effort of throwing the ball helps participants find a sense of literally throwing the voice with confidence.

## Further development

1 Once the group is familiar with the exercise, remove the ball and repeat the exercise using an imaginary, mimed ball. The aim is to keep the positive effect of the voice without being dependent on the ball.

2 The group breaks into two sub-groups who practise speaking an easy-to-remember nursery rhyme together, so that they can recite it clearly. The two sub-groups go to opposite ends of the room and, one at a time, recite their rhymes with a sense of projecting the words all the way to the other group as audience.

# Makaton story/poem

## Preparation

A picture or a couple of puppets are introduced to the group to stimulate ideas for a simple story or poem.

## Activity

The group leader elicits ideas for a story from the group. The story grows line by line, by group agreement. As each line is agreed upon it is illustrated by Makaton signs, enhanced by simple mime gestures and facial expressions. The group learns each line and repeats it several times, signing and reciting all together at the same time. The story can be recapped and gradually extended over a series of sessions until a natural ending is found. The whole piece can become a short choral performance project.

## Purpose

The project is a creative, enjoyable application of Makaton, a sign language system devised specifically for people with learning difficulties. It is very much a group activity and provides a sense of group achievement.

## Further development

The same process can be used to tell a story from history, or from the personal history of the group.

*Makaton is a structured language programme which uses speech, manual signs and graphic symbols. It is used extensively in the UK and many other countries. It is important to note that because the signs matched to the Makaton Programme are from the sign language used for deaf people they will differ in each country. The website for the Makaton charity in the UK is* https://www.makaton.org, *where you can find details of training and other resources.*

VOICE WORK 4

# Vocal orchestra

## Preparation

Make sure that the group is broadly familiar with the appearance and sound of a variety of musical instruments found in the orchestra. This could be done through looking at pictures of instruments while listening to pre-recorded music, watching a video of an orchestra playing, or attending a live concert.

## Activity

The group leader takes the group through a series of musical mimes illustrated by the voice. Possible instruments include violin, cello, double bass, trombone, trumpet, flute, piano, harp and gong. The sounds produced can use the whole range of the voice, and do not have to be musically pleasing. The group breaks into two sub-groups, each group 'playing' a particular instrument. A musical dialogue develops as an improvisation and is brought to a conclusion.

## Purpose

The exercise can be used as a way of working on awareness of sound and music. The individual sounds of the various instruments encourage a non-habitual use of the voice, and development of spontaneity.

## Further development

1 Explore short musical dialogues in pairs, where each person chooses his own instrument. The group listens as each pair has the chance to create a sound mime duet. Partners should maintain an attentiveness to each other so that they are always in contact. They can remain stationary or move around the space with their imaginary instruments, coming closer and moving further away as their feeling demands.

2 Opera improvisation: everyone chooses a sentence they can remember and repeat; the whole group sings each sentence as if they are opera singers. They should use gesture and try to sing with feeling and a sense of drama. In pairs, they practise operatic dialogues, each person using only their chosen sentence.

# Group hum

## Preparation

The group creates a circle which allows everyone to be in physical contact with each other comfortably. Let the group decide on the kind of circle: perhaps holding hands at some distance, arms over shoulders to create a group huddle or sitting on the floor facing outwards with arms, sides and backs touching. They need to be close enough to allow everyone to listen carefully while respecting individual needs for physical space.

## Activity

Everyone is invited to close their eyes and to listen to the silence in the room and the sound of breathing. Someone starts to hum and gradually everyone joins in. They concentrate on the sound created by the group as a whole. The volume and the notes may change. The group brings the improvised hum to a natural end.

## Purpose

The exercise promotes sensitive listening. Each person is able to contribute to a whole group effect without being isolated and can develop confidence in using the voice. It can be a relaxing way to close a session (see *Chapter 13*, on closures).

## Further development

Extend the exercise to include experiments with additional vowel and percussive sounds created with the voice, hands, body and floor. Maintain the emphasis on listening to the group as a whole.

# CHAPTER 5

# Life Skills Role-Play

# Warm-up for life skills role-play

Before embarking on a role-play, make sure the group is warmed up. The warm-up should address three levels. The first level is **finding a way of being together as a group in a spirit of playfulness and creativity.** A selection of activities from *Chapters 1, 2* and *4* can be used. The second level is **awakening an interest in the theme of the role-play.** This can be achieved with a short introductory talk and discussion conducted by the group leader, or an interview whereby the group leader asks each participant in turn some questions relating to the theme, such as "Would you tell us about your experiences of travelling by bus?" **Preparing group members to take on and stay in role for a while** is the third level. Before asking group members to take on roles individually, the group leader may take them through some preparatory characterization exercises as a whole group. Each main role in the role-play can be played at first by the group as a whole. For example, "All practise the role of bus driver or conductor. What does she say as you get on the bus? How does she sit? All practise the role of a passenger. What do you say as you get on the bus? What do you give the driver, and what does he give you? If you have a pass where do you tap it?" In this way the group prepares a skeleton action or dialogue, which is fleshed out in more detail in the role-play. Everyone gets a taste of each role, regardless of which role they go on to play more fully.

Any situation can be dramatized and practised through role-play. The following selection is grouped into four sample categories: (a) shops and services, (b) doctors and dentists, (c) transport, and (d) household and personal skills. The level of challenge and detail worked towards should be appropriate to the age and ability of the group. The role-play may be used to practise complex verbal exchanges and social interaction or as a way of familiarizing participants in advance with a new situation. Group members may benefit from taking part either actively or passively within the role-play.

# Shops and services

## Money quiz

### Preparation

The group looks at and handles some real money, and identifies a range of common notes and coins. Numbers, words, pictures, size and shape can all help in identifying the different denominations.

### Activity

The quiz itself focuses on identification of different coins and notes, and on recognizing relative value. The group leader takes on the role of quizmaster and the group splits into two teams of equal size. The team may discuss each question before giving an answer.

*Round 1*: "What's this note worth?" In turn, each team is given a note to identity.

*Round 2*: "What's this coin worth?" Each team gets a coin to identify.

*Round 3*: individual questions. Each individual in each team is given a coin or note to identify, if possible without help from the rest of the team.

*Round 4*: putting in order of value. Each team is given the same series of coins and notes. The group task is to lay them side by side in order of value, the most valuable at one end, the least valuable at the other.

*Round 5*: "Not enough!" or "Don't forget your change!" The quizmaster approaches each team as if intending to buy an item. She names the item and hands over a note or coin: for example, "I'd like to buy that DVD. Here's £20." The team has to decide whether she needs to pay more or is owed some change, responding either with "Not enough!" or "Don't forget your change!"

### Purpose

The quiz provides a fun format for familiarization with money. It is useful to be able to recognize different denominations and have a general sense of value, even if exact adding and subtraction skills are limited. The quiz can be repeated over a period of time.

# Shops and services

## Further development

1  Each correct answer can be scored on a board. When the points are added, the teams can discuss what they would buy if each point were a penny, a pound or a thousand pounds. This could give the starting point for a subsequent roleplay, such as buying sweets, clothes or a car. See the next exercise ('Going Shopping: Making Choices').

2  Before a holiday overseas, use this exercise to introduce foreign currency.

# Shops and services

*continued from previous page*

## Going shopping: Making choices

### Preparation

Introduce the idea of going shopping. Ask the group to choose the kind of shop. A selection of props and costumes should be at hand.

### Activity

Begin as a whole group by setting the scene physically in the space, using chairs, blocks, cloths, etc. Clarify where the entrance is, how the wares are laid out in the shop, and where the counter is. The scene may be based on an actual shop known by group members. Decide as a group what roles are needed to people the scene: shop assistants, manager, customers and so on.

Get into role. Each person chooses what role they will play, and uses costume or props to clarify this. A brief interview in role with the group leader follows to clarify their intention in the scene. For example: "You're a customer? What are you hoping to buy today?" or "You're a shop assistant? What do you have to do in your work?" The group leader invites the 'staff' on to the acting area first, then one or more 'customers'. Allow the scene to run freely for a while so that the atmosphere of the shop is built up, and participants can settle into their roles.

The group leader guides the focus to the theme of making choices. Perhaps it is a question of deciding between three pullovers according to size, colour and price. Here are two possible exchanges:

CUSTOMER: What size is this one?
ASSISTANT: Let me see . . . medium.
CUSTOMER: Can I try it on?
ASSISTANT: Yes. The changing rooms are over there.
CUSTOMER: (after trying on the pullover) It's too small. Do you have a larger one?

CUSTOMER: How much is this blue one?
ASSISTANT: £40
CUSTOMER: And this brown one?

Assistant: £30

Customer: They both fit me. I prefer the blue one for £40, but then I won't have any money left for gloves. . .

● At the point where the customer has to make their choice, the group leader may stop the action and ask the group as a whole what the customer's options are and what they would do. Returning to the scene, the customer makes a choice, perhaps buying the pullover, perhaps deciding to go away and think about it or come back with a friend. The focus moves on to the next customer.

Throughout these scenes each main character can be 'doubled' or accompanied by the group leader or member of the staff team if necessary to prompt and give support.

## Purpose

The role-play serves the general purpose of familiarizing participants with the various transactions involved in going shopping. The group leader can use it to draw attention to specific issues, such as budgeting.

## Further development

1 The role-play has so many variations that it is worth returning to it several times. Make sure that participants who play the role of shop staff also get the chance to play the role of customer and vice versa.

2 One interaction can be followed up like a continuing story. For example, the customer buys the pullover without trying it on. When she gets home she decides it does not suit her and takes it back. (See next exercise, 'Going Shopping: Taking Something Back'.)

# Shops and services

continued from previous page

### Going shopping: Taking something back

#### Preparation

Props are needed to represent wares in a shop; also a bag or box with the product to be returned, a piece of paper to represent a receipt, and money. Begin with a discussion in the group about people's experiences of buying something and it not working, not fitting, or their not being happy with it for some other reason. The scene can be based on one of these stories or products, or a hypothetical situation.

#### Activity

The role-play takes place in two scenes. Both scenes can be set up simply by the whole group in the acting area: first, at home, where the decision is made to take an item back to the shop; second, the shop itself. Roles are identified and allocated by the group, such as customer and friend at home, shop assistant and manager at the shop. Costumes and props are used simply as necessary to define roles. Those group members without a role have the function of advisers and supporters. They can make suggestions to the actors and even show them how they might deal with the same situation.

In the first scene, the customer shows his friend what he has just bought, perhaps a new pullover. Trying it on, he realizes the sleeves are too short. The friend's task is to help him prepare to take it back and change it. Possible dialogue:

CUSTOMER: It's too small, isn't it?
FRIEND: Yes. You should take it back.
CUSTOMER: I've never done that before; what do I need to do?
FRIEND/GROUP ADVISERS: Take it off, fold it and put it in its bag! Find your receipt. Go to the shop and explain. I'll come with you and help.

The second scene addresses the need to find the right person to talk to, getting the message across clearly and the importance of receipts. Possible dialogue:

CUSTOMER: Let's find a shop assistant.
FRIEND: There's one at the till over there.

LIFE SKILLS ROLE-PLAY

# Shops and services

CUSTOMER: I bought this pullover this morning, and it doesn't fit. I'd like my money back.

ASSISTANT: I can't really do that.

FRIEND/GROUP ADVISERS: Tell him you've got a receipt. Ask for the manager.

CUSTOMER: I'd like to speak to the manager, please.

ASSISTANT: I'll get her.

MANAGER: What seems to be the problem?

CUSTOMER: I bought this pullover this morning, and it doesn't fit. I'd like my money back.

MANAGER: Well, if you've got a receipt there should be no problem with that. Let me have a look at the pullover. Yes, that looks all right. Are you sure you wouldn't like another pullover?

CUSTOMER: No, I'd rather have my money back, thanks.

MANAGER: Can I have the receipt then, please?

CUSTOMER: Here.

MANAGER: And here's your £30. Good afternoon!

CUSTOMER AND FRIEND: Goodbye!

FRIEND: Shall we have a look in another shop while we're in town?

## Purpose

The role-play is a useful exercise in assertiveness and persistence. It also demonstrates the importance of preparation when approaching a challenging task.

# Shops and services

*continued from previous page*

## At the hairdressers

### Preparation

Introduce the theme of going to the hairdressers. Discuss group members' experiences of going to the hairdressers, what they enjoy and what they don't like. Make a list of possible services available, together with prices, on a large card. Props and cloths are needed to represent bottles, towels, overalls, combs, scissors, magazines and so on. A real mirror is useful.

### Activity

The group starts by setting up together the salon, with an entrance, reception desk, wash basins and an area for styling. Identify the roles: receptionist, hair washer, stylist, someone sweeping up, customers. Group members choose which roles they will play, and prepare themselves with costume and props.

The focus of the role play may be what to say when arriving at the salon; making a choice of service according to taste and price; speaking up when something is not right; paying for the service. Possible dialogues might go as follows:

RECEPTIONIST: Can I help you?
CUSTOMER: I'd like to have my hair done, please.
RECEPTIONIST: Do you have an appointment?
CUSTOMER: No.
RECEPTIONIST: Well, we're busy now, but I can fit you in tomorrow morning.

CUSTOMER: I've found a picture in this magazine. I'd like it like this.
STYLIST: I can do that, but it means having a tint.
CUSTOMER: What would it cost?
STYLIST: An extra £40.
CUSTOMER: That's too much for me. What else can you suggest?

HAIR WASHER: Is the water all right for you?
CUSTOMER: It's a bit hot.
HAIR WASHER: How is it now?
CUSTOMER: It's still too hot.

*LIFE SKILLS ROLE-PLAY*

---

# Shops and services

*continued from previous page*

## At the hairdressers

### Preparation

Introduce the theme of going to the hairdressers. Discuss group members' experiences of going to the hairdressers, what they enjoy and what they don't like. Make a list of possible services available, together with prices, on a large card. Props and cloths are needed to represent bottles, towels, overalls, combs, scissors, magazines and so on. A real mirror is useful.

### Activity

The group starts by setting up together the salon, with an entrance, reception desk, wash basins and an area for styling. Identify the roles: receptionist, hair washer, stylist, someone sweeping up, customers. Group members choose which roles they will play, and prepare themselves with costume and props.

The focus of the role play may be what to say when arriving at the salon; making a choice of service according to taste and price; speaking up when something is not right; paying for the service. Possible dialogues might go as follows:

RECEPTIONIST: Can I help you?
CUSTOMER: I'd like to have my hair done, please.
RECEPTIONIST: Do you have an appointment?
CUSTOMER: No.
RECEPTIONIST: Well, we're busy now, but I can fit you in tomorrow morning.

CUSTOMER: I've found a picture in this magazine. I'd like it like this.
STYLIST: I can do that, but it means having a tint.
CUSTOMER: What would it cost?
STYLIST: An extra £40.
CUSTOMER: That's too much for me. What else can you suggest?

HAIR WASHER: Is the water all right for you?
CUSTOMER: It's a bit hot.
HAIR WASHER: How is it now?
CUSTOMER: It's still too hot.

*5 LIFE SKILLS ROLE-PLAY*

116

CREATIVE DRAMA GROUPWORK FOR PEOPLE WITH LEARNING DIFFICULTIES

Copyright material from Anna Chesner (2020), *Creative Drama Groupwork for People with Learning Difficulties*, Routledge

HAIR WASHER: Now?
CUSTOMER: That's better, thanks.

RECEPTIONIST: That'll be £24.99 please. How would you like to pay? Cash, cheque, credit card?
CUSTOMER: Cash, here's £40.
RECEPTIONIST: Thank you very much, and here's your change.

## Purpose

The role-play can help participants gain confidence in going to the hairdressers independently. It also gives an insight into the different tasks involved for those working there.

## Further development

Develop the theme of self-presentation and self-care with further discussions or role-plays around fashion, taste and personal grooming. Pictures in magazines provide a useful starting point for discussion.

LIFE SKILLS ROLE-PLAY

# Shops and services

*continued from previous page*

## Eating out

### Preparation

Introduce the theme of eating out and the variety of establishments people go to, from fast food self-service chains to waiter service restaurants. Pass around a selection of paper, plastic and china cups and plates. Identify as a group which kind of establishment these objects come from, and what kind of food or drink might be served in them. A selection of props, such as tablecloths, napkins, menus and trays, is useful.

### Activity

As a group, set the scene of a restaurant or cafe, with entrance, tables, menus and kitchen area. Identify the roles: customers, waiters and kitchen staff. Group members choose which role they will play, and prepare with costume and props.

The focus of the role-play may be choosing from a menu and placing an order; paying; making conversation at table. Some starting points for exchanges follow.

WAITER: Are you ready to order now?

CUSTOMER(s): That was delicious. We should go now. Waiter, we'd like to pay.

CUSTOMER A: How's your pasta?
CUSTOMER B: Good; thanks; very filling.
CUSTOMER A: Are you having a dessert?
CUSTOMER B: No, but I might have a coffee.
CUSTOMER A: I wonder what sort of ice cream they do.

### Purpose

The role-play provides a practice situation in which participants can familiarize themselves with some of the rituals and the atmosphere of eating out.

### Further development

Go out to a real cafe or restaurant as a group.

# Doctors and dentists

## The doctor's waiting room

### Preparation

Introduce the theme of going to the doctor. Invite group members to name their own family doctor. Gather spontaneous ideas about some of the reasons people go to the doctor: checkups, injections, illnesses, getting prescriptions, and so on. Leaflets, a white coat, toys, pen and paper a computer and a clock are useful props.

### Activity

Set the scene as a group: a reception and waiting area, with magazines, leaflets, toys, clock, 'no smoking' sign. Identify the different roles: receptionist, doctor, nurse practitioners, patients of various ages, with different reasons for coming – some with appointments, some without. Everyone chooses a role, and adopts props and costume as appropriate.

As each character enters the action area, the receptionist checks their name and appointment time, and sends them to the waiting area. What happens in the waiting area is up to the participants. They may or may not choose to talk to each other, read magazines and leaflets or play with toys. From time to time a patient is called through to the doctor, perhaps accompanied by an electronic buzz and the name appearing on the electronic noticeboard. If there is not much spontaneous interaction in the waiting room, the group leader can interview each person in role. In this way the unspoken thoughts and feelings of the characters, such as discomfort, anxiety and impatience, are heard.

### Purpose

Participants can familiarize themselves with the ritual of going to the doctor. Particular issues can be addressed, such as having to wait, dealing with the doctor running late, or making conversation.

### Further development

1 The same format can be used to explore going to the hospital.

CREATIVE DRAMA GROUPWORK FOR PEOPLE WITH LEARNING DIFFICULTIES ⋯⋯⋯ 119

Copyright material from Anna Chesner (2020), *Creative Drama Groupwork for People with Learning Difficulties*, Routledge

LIFE SKILLS ROLE-PLAY 5

# Doctors and dentists

● ● ● ● ● ● ● ● ● ● ● ● ● ● ● ● ● ● ● ● ● ● ● ● ● ● ● ● ● ● ● ● ● ● ● ● ● ● ● ● ● ● ● ●

*continued from previous page*

**2** A subsequent scene can be used to practise describing symptoms to the doctor. Each patient is called through to the doctor one at a time and is asked, "What seems to be the matter?" The patient replies, and the doctor's response may be to give an examination, write a prescription, send the patient home with a clean bill of health, ask them to make another appointment, or refer them on to a specialist. The group leader can double the role of either the patient or the doctor, if necessary, acting as a kind of prompt.

## Making an appointment

### Preparation

Two telephones are required. Introduce the idea of making an appointment to see the doctor or dentist.

### Activity

Each group member has a turn at telephoning to make an appointment, and at being the receptionist receiving the phone call. The group has the chance to give helpful critical feedback in terms of volume and clarity. The first stage involves getting through, dialling the number and identifying the ringing or engaged tone, as provided by the group in chorus. The second stage, the conversation, may involve a dialogue such as the following:

RECEPTIONIST: Ball and de Souza dental practice. How can I help you?
CALLER: This is Fred Mitchum. I'm a patient of Mr. de Souza. I'd like to make an appointment, please.
RECEPTIONIST: I can offer you this Friday at 11 o'clock.
CALLER: Fine, thank you. This Friday at 11 o'clock.
RECEPTIONIST: Right, Mr. Mitchum. Friday the twentieth at 11 o'clock. Goodbye.
CALLER: Goodbye.

The last stage is group feedback. If the caller was too quiet, too fast or indistinct, the group can suggest an action replay of all or part of the phone call, with a chance for the caller to improve their delivery.

# Doctors and dentists

## Purpose

The role-play provides general practice in telephone skills, and specific practice in making a medical/dental appointment.

## Further development

1 Follow up by using a real phone, perhaps to a member of the staff team, for a social conversation.

2 If a group member needs to make an actual appointment, give them the opportunity to do it in the group with the support of the group members, after having first practised through role-play.

# Transport

## Catching the right bus

### Preparation

Have some large pieces of card and felt pens ready.

### Activity

Introduce the theme of travelling by bus. Where do group members travel to by bus? Which bus stop do they use and which number do they have to look out for? Write the relevant bus numbers on the pieces of card, along with one or two that are not relevant.

Set up a simple roadside scene, with a road and a bus stop. Some of the group take on the role of people waiting for the bus, and the others take on the role of individual buses, holding their number in front of them. As each bus comes along, the people at the bus stop have to identify the number, either by reading it or by asking someone. When the right bus comes along, they flag it down and ride off behind the bus driver. Other buses they ignore, letting them go by, or watching other passengers board.

The scene is repeated with a change of roles, so that those who played the part of buses are now passengers and vice versa.

### Purpose

The scene is essentially a game of identification, in which group members practise recognizing the right bus and, if necessary, getting help to do so.

### Further development

As each person gets on their bus, they tell the driver their destination and buy their ticket. Or buy their ticket at a machine prior to boarding. In the case of a pass or Oyster card, they need to get this ready for touching in or showing. If necessary, set some time aside to practise asking for the destinations before the scene is set up.

CREATIVE DRAMA GROUPWORK FOR PEOPLE WITH LEARNING DIFFICULTIES

# Transport

## Getting to know a route

This role-play is of particular relevance when group members are beginning to travel independently or are getting to know a new route.

### Preparation

Make sure there is plenty of free space to work in, and a variety of objects to hand to build the scene.

### Activity

The group builds the various landmarks for a particular journey in the drama space. A chair, box or lamp stand draped in a cloth may represent particular places visible on a bus journey, or particular stations on a train journey. Begin with the starting point for the journey, such as home or the local bus stop, and end with the destination. Once the scene is set, the group as a whole journeys through it, naming the particular places they are passing. Then repeat the journey in pairs, and as individuals if relevant.

### Purpose

The repetition of this role-play can help build confidence in making a journey independently. The challenge increases gradually as the journey is undertaken first by the whole group, then pairs and then individuals.

### Further development

The same method can be used for more complex journeys, where it is necessary to change buses, or use a combination of modes of transport. The whole sequence can be mapped out in advance and practised on a small scale in the drama group.

# Transport

∙∙∙∙∙∙∙∙∙∙∙∙∙∙∙∙∙∙∙∙∙∙∙∙∙∙∙∙∙∙∙∙∙∙∙∙∙∙∙∙∙∙∙∙∙∙∙∙∙∙∙∙∙∙

*continued from previous page*

## Travelling by plane

This role-play is of particular relevance as a preparation for a journey by plane.

### Preparation

Introduce the topic of travelling by plane by means of pictures and discussion. Elicit ideas from the group about what they will need to take with them, such as passports, tickets, travelling bags and money. Allocate props to represent these items.

### Activity

The role-play is structured in three scenes, each of which can be set up as needed. Participants can choose their roles before each scene and adopt appropriate props or pieces of costume. The first scene is at the airport. Passengers queue at the check-in desk, show their tickets and passports, get their luggage weighed, hand it over and receive their boarding pass. They then pass through hand luggage and passport control, and are called to a boarding gate.

The second scene is on the plane. The passengers board the plane, find their places and observe the 'no smoking' and 'fasten your seat belt' signs. They are greeted by cabin crew and watch the safety demonstration. The plane takes off, then they are served with a drink and a meal. Eventually the plane comes in to land. The group can make the sounds of the plane taking off and landing in chorus.

The third scene is at the destination airport. In this scene everyone shows their passport at passport control. Baggage is picked up and everyone leaves the airport for the final destination.

### Purpose

The role-play can be used to familiarize participants with the different stages of travelling by plane, to reduce anxiety before a journey and to increase understanding of travelling by air.

# Transport

### Further development

As well as serving as preparation for a journey, the role-play can be adapted as a means of remembering an actual journey undertaken by the whole group or by one group member who can share some of the experience with the rest of the group (see *Chapter 9,* on dramatization).

LIFE SKILLS ROLE-PLAY

# Household and personal skills

## What's cooking?

### Preparation

Ask the group what food they like eating and what they can prepare themselves. An apron or two can be useful to identify the role of cook(s). Some plain coloured cloths may also be used to help identify further roles.

### Activity

A volunteer or volunteer couple from the group take on the role of cooks. The rest of the group are used as ingredients, and may drape themselves in appropriate coloured cloths as their specific roles are identified. They are stirred together, sprinkled and made to sizzle and rise according to the menu. Sound effects are welcome. Any known meal or dish can be prepared in this way, and new fantasy dishes can be created.

### Purpose

This role-play can be used to back up a particular skill learned in cookery. It is also fun and helps a group to bond.

### Further development

The same principle can be followed to practise laying a table or washing up. Group members take on the role of cutlery, washing bowl and so on.

LIFE SKILLS ROLE-PLAY

5

# Household and personal skills

## Show me how!

### Preparation

Gather spontaneous ideas about the different everyday skills group members use during the course of a day, such as making the bed, getting dressed, preparing breakfast, clearing up, cleaning a floor, using a music system, crossing a road or going shopping.

### Activity

Each group member shows the group how they do one everyday activity. They can mime it, use props or other group members to show how it is done, and give a commentary, describing what they are doing. The rest of the group watches and those who want to can try the action out for themselves.

### Purpose

The role-play is primarily a confidence builder, giving participants the awareness that they have valuable skills.

### Further development

1 Leave out the commentary until the group guesses what the activity is.

2 When group members are mastering a new skill, the role-play can be used for mutual support and co-operative learning. Here a sub-group or the group as a whole works together, each member contributing what they remember or know.

CHAPTER 6

# Games

Games are at the heart of social interaction, providing a basic structure with rules, whilst also being an opportunity for each person to express and take their place in their own particular way.

# Pass the squeeze

## Activity

The group sits in a circle holding hands. Everyone closes their eyes and the group leader squeezes the hand of the person to her left. That person passes the squeeze on to the person to their left, and so on until the squeeze returns to the group leader. The same exercise is repeated to the right. If necessary, do the first round with the eyes open so that the whole group can see the squeeze going round. Then do it with the eyes closed, with the emphasis on feeling and sensation.

## Purpose

This is a concentration and co-ordination game, equally accessible to non-verbal and verbal group members. It works well both as a preparation for further work requiring concentration and as a wind-down after more boisterous or noisy activity (see *Chapter 13*, on closures).

## Further development

1 If the group has mastered the basic game, try introducing a sequence of squeezes, such as two short squeezes and a long one.

2 Introduce a new rule, whereby anyone can change the direction of the squeeze when it is their turn, simply by repeating the squeeze with the hand they have received with.

3 The group leader sends two squeezes round the circle in opposite directions at the same time. Someone will be the crossover point.

# The name–place game

## Preparation

A hand-held percussive instrument, such as a tambourine or gong, is required.

## Activity

The group begins by making a large, standing circle. If it is difficult to keep a sense of the circle, try holding hands first to concretize it. Take a moment to look around and notice who else is in the group. The group leader has the gong or tambourine and may take it round the group, giving each person a chance to strike it once and hear its sound. This sound will be the cue for two people to change places in the circle. The sequence is as follows:

1 The group leader calls out the names of two people in the group.

2 These two locate each other and make eye contact. A moment of anticipation, until. . .

3 The gong is struck and they cross the circle to exchange places.

The game continues until everybody has changed places several times.

## Purpose

In its simplest form, this game demands awareness of self and others in the group, concentration and directional movement. It encourages a sense of self in space.

## Further development

1 As participants cross paths in the circle, they find a way to greet each other, such as a wave, hug, handshake or some other spontaneous gesture.

2 In a second round, or when the game is very familiar, each pair is given a 'feeling' word to express in their manner of moving across the space. For example, the group leader says, "Tomas and Alina, change places, but this time as if you were feeling very tired [angry/sad/happy]."

3 Pass the leadership and the gong to a group member who then gets to choose two people, call their names (or point them out) and determine the moment they are to cross the circle by striking the gong.

# Introduction game

## Activity

Everyone stands in a circle, with the group leader in the middle. She approaches someone in the circle and introduces herself: "I'm Anna." The person approached responds with his name: "I'm Tomas." They shake hands, and change places. Tomas now goes into the middle and chooses someone to introduce himself to, and so on until everyone has had at least one go in the middle.

## Purpose

Introducing oneself is a social skill that may be practised in this game. It also gives the opportunity to remember names, to choose and be chosen. The movement pattern demands concentration, and there is group satisfaction as it is mastered.

## Further development

Everyone chooses a famous person and introduces themselves as that person. The mode of greeting changes accordingly. How does the Queen of England shake hands? How does Stormzy walk as he approaches someone? This variation moves the game into the realm of role-play (see *Chapter 8,* on improvisation).

# Observation game

## Activity

Group members stand or sit in a circle and take a moment to look at each other, taking particular note of what people are wearing. The group leader chooses a visual criterion and asks any people with that criterion to change places (for example, anyone with black trainers on, wearing earrings, wearing something blue, with red hair and so on). Start with something that only applies to two people, as this is simpler. Later in the game, try something more complex, with three people or more changing places. Those who do not fit the criterion can prompt those who do. At the end call out something that applies to everyone, so there is a moment of general excitement as everyone changes places.

## Purpose

As its name suggests, the function of this game is to increase observation skills. It is particularly useful with people who tend to be so occupied with themselves that they hardly notice others.

## Further development

1 Ask the group for ideas for the next round. This could be as simple as a particular colour or item of clothing to be called out.

2 Instead of asking about what can be observed, the game can be used to find out more about each other, such as who has a brother, who has a birthday in May or who likes scrambled egg.

# Musical find your space

## Preparation

A ball is required, and a source of music, electronic or live.

## Activity

The group stands in a large circle, and a ball or other object is introduced. When the music plays the ball is passed from person to person around the circle. When the music stops, whoever is holding the ball stops and places the ball on the floor in front of their feet. They leave it there and go for a walk around the outside of the circle until they return to their original place and pick up the ball. When the music starts they pass the ball on, and the game continues.

## Purpose

The game is a simplified version of 'Journey Round the World' (see below). The ball concretizes the empty place, which makes it easier to identity.

# Journey round the world

## Preparation

A hat is needed, preferably one evocative of adventure and travel. Alternatively, a small, light rucksack or suitcase will do.

## Activity

The group creates a large standing circle, perhaps by holding hands. It is important that everybody has a sense of their place in the circle, so the group leader encourages everyone to take a moment to notice where their place is, who is on either side, who is opposite and so on. One person is given the hat and is 'the traveller'. They can wear the hat or just carry it. They leave their place, 'home', and set off on a journey round the outside of the circle. This is seen imaginatively as an epic journey round the world. The group can wave them goodbye as they set off, wish them luck and watch their progress. The traveller's journey is complete when they find their place again, the gap in the circle left by their departure. The group can give help or encouragement, if necessary, and welcome the traveller as they arrive back home. The travelling hat is passed to someone else and another round commences.

## Purpose

The image of a solitary journey undertaken and completed brings to mind the great adventures of epic heroes. Here the journey is safe and physically very defined, but there is a sense of satisfaction in successfully completing the journey, and in being recognized for the achievement by the group. At the same time, the game demands observation skills and promotes an awareness of space.

## Further development

As the traveller passes behind each of the other members of the group, they can make contact in some way. At a basic level this may be a touch or quiet greeting. Or each person may take on the role of a country or town somewhere en route. As they are passed and touched, they announce themselves, and the group leader can incorporate this into a narrative of the journey. For example:

# Journey round the world

GROUP LEADER: Maya is making her way from Italy now and is arriving at . . .

GROUP MEMBER: I'm Alaska.

GROUP LEADER: She's arrived in Alaska. Yes, it's getting very cold on this part of the journey, look at all that snow, but it can't be long before Maya arrives home. She's made her way through Alaska and is now approaching. . .

**NB** Geographical consistency is of course less important here than the sense of the journey, however fantastical.

# The calling game

## Preparation

As much space as possible is needed in this game, so furniture and props should be moved to the sides of the room. The game is easier to manage with a staff member or helper.

## Activity

The group leader stands at one end of the room, facing away from the group. Everyone stands in a line at the other end of the room facing the group leader's back. A helper makes sure everyone is in line. The group leader calls "Ready!" and this is the cue for everyone in the line to call "Hello!", if necessary with the added encouragement of the helper. The group leader turns round and calls the name of the first person she heard, and invites them to step forward one, two or three steps, or to come forward an equivalent distance with a wheelchair. The helper monitors this if necessary. The round ends when one group member gets close enough to the group leader to tap her on the back. Having won the round, they get a moment of applause, perhaps a small prize, and the opportunity to take on the role that the group leader had in the first round. They may also choose to share this role with the group leader or helper if they need support with fulfilling the sequence.

## Purpose

The game helps with verbal articulation and voice projection (see *Chapter 4*, on voice work). It encourages players to make themselves heard. Often people with learning difficulties have a history of repeatedly being told to be quiet, which leads to a lack of confidence in the use of the voice. Through activities such as these they can regain some confidence. Those who, because of their difficulty, need a longer time to formulate their words may also lose confidence, and this may be reflected in a quiet voice and a reluctance to compete to be heard. In this game they can be encouraged by a helper by use of eye contact or gentle prompting to get over this hurdle and fill the room with the sound of their own voice. The game also provides an opportunity to practise counting, as steps are taken, and there can be a physical focus, as participants are encouraged to take long, purposeful strides.

# The calling game

## Further development

For the more verbally proficient group, change the word "Hello" to a longer phrase, such as "Turn round, Anna!" (substitute the name of whoever is at the front) or, more playfully, "Guess who's coming to dinner!"

# Dice game

## Preparation

A large cubic dice is needed, about 20 cm (8 inches) high. Foam dice of this type can be bought from toy shops or online.

## Activity

Each person throws the dice once. The number they throw becomes their number, unless it is already taken, in which case they throw again. If there are more than six in the group, two or more people can have the same number. When everyone has a number to identify with, one person throws the dice again. The group calls out the number and works out whose number it is. Whoever it applies to gets to throw the next number.

## Purpose

The use of the dice encourages observation and familiarity with numbers. There is also a chance for each person to be a performer and the centre of attention for a moment.

## Further development

1 Instead of just throwing the dice, the chosen group member can also take a bow or perform a sound or movement of their choice. This can develop into a short song, dance or musical performance.

2 The chosen person becomes the group leader for a minute and teaches the group a favourite physical exercise or dance movement.

# The imagination game

## Preparation

A large cloth is required.

## Activity

The group stands or sits in a circle. One person takes the cloth and moves with it, or uses it as if it were something else. This is easier to model than to explain verbally. The possibilities are extensive: the wings of a bird, a hat, a cloud, a baby, a cake, a sail, and so on. The group guesses what the cloth represents, and it is passed to the next person, who transforms it and uses it in a new way.

## Purpose

This game exercises the imagination and spontaneity (see *Chapter 8*, on improvisation). If at first these qualities are lacking in a group, it is fine for group members all to use the same idea, or to copy ideas of the group leader. It can be a shared group task to find a fresh idea.

## Further development

1 Try the same idea but with a cloth of different colour, size or texture; or with a different kind of object, such as a ball.

2 Pass around a shoe box, or shopping bag. Each person opens it, reaches in and pulls out an invisible, imaginary object which they show the group. They can indicate what it is through mime, or tell the group what they have found.

# Where's the mouse?

## Preparation

A toy mouse is needed: a small bean bag can be transformed by painting on a mouse face and sewing on a tail.

## Activity

One person stands in the middle of the circle. The toy mouse is passed around the circle as unobtrusively as possible, behind the back, from hand to hand, or with the feet. The one in the middle points when she sees it, at which point she joins the circle and chooses the next person to go in the middle.

## Purpose

Co-ordination and group co-operation are needed to keep the mouse hidden. Sophisticated players will find subtle ways to distract the attention from where the real action is. For the person in the middle, the game provides a challenge and the chance to pit their observation skills against the group.

## Further development

The person in the centre takes on the role of cat, and wears a suitable piece of costume. This can be a tail, whiskers on elastic, paw-like mittens, or a hat with a cat design on it. The moment they see the mouse they meow and do a stylized pounce in the direction of the mouse.

# Hidden treasure

## Preparation

Some 'treasure' is required. This should be about the size of a tennis ball, and something without sharp edges. For example, you can use a ball, an orange, a bead necklace, a purse or a small ornament.

## Activity

First, the object is passed around the group, so that everyone has a chance to explore it. The group leader explains that it is valuable treasure, and asks the group for suggestions where it might have come from. If the group does not manage to come up with suggestions, she offers alternatives; for example, it might have been stolen from the Tower of London, found in the garden or street, or washed ashore after a shipwreck. Once the group has agreed on the origin of the treasure, a volunteer is required to be the treasure hunter. This person leaves the room for a few moments, perhaps escorted by a helper. During this time, one group member hides the treasure somewhere on their person. Good places are inside the top of a sock, peeping out of a cuff or in a hood. The group calls "Ready!" and the treasure hunter comes in, with the task of finding out who has the treasure. This may involve taking a close look at everyone, as he walks around the group, or gently 'frisking' the 'suspects' until the treasure is found.

## Purpose

This game has strong elements of imagination and role-play and can be used as the main activity in the development part of a session. As well as being fun, there are a number of issues that can be worked on. First, the idea of keeping a secret often comes up when playing this game. Some players may be more keen to be 'helpful' and show the treasure hunter where the treasure is than to hold on to their secret knowledge and watch the treasure hunter struggle.

Second, the issue of personal space comes up when the search moves on to a physical level. The game gives a good opportunity to encourage awareness, sensitivity and respect around physical contact.

GAMES 6

# Hidden treasure

● ● ● ● ● ● ● ● ● ● ● ● ● ● ● ● ● ● ● ● ● ● ● ● ● ● ● ● ● ● ● ● ● ● ● ● ● ● ● ●

*continued from previous page*

Finally, in terms of a continuing creative drama group, this game prepares participants to make believe, both in terms of the object representing treasure, and in terms of the dramatic role of treasure hunter.

## Further development

1 Use the game as the basis for a dramatized story on the same theme, where each participant has an imaginary role. Maybe base it on some version of *Pirates of the Caribbean*.

2 The treasure is hidden in the room, not on someone's person. The treasure hunters are guided to it by the group calling out "Warmer!" as they get closer, or "Colder!" as they move away.

# The mime game

## Preparation

The group leader introduces a number of simple mimes, representing possible scenes from everyday life, such as the following:

waking up, yawning, rubbing eyes and stretching, brushing teeth, washing or taking a shower, getting dressed, tying a shoe lace, drinking coffee, peeling and eating a banana, driving a car, reading a book, digging the garden, painting a picture, having a chat, dancing, watching television, going to sleep.

- The group goes through this sequence together, although each person can perform the mime in their own way.

## Activity

In turn, each person tells the group a story in mime, by putting together any of the mimes practised and adding any new ones that fit the story and come to mind. The group leader gives support by being the narrator and describing in words what the mime is showing the group. The story can be as short or as long as the performer feels comfortable with.

## Purpose

This game introduces the group to the idea of a dramatic language. It is equally accessible to verbal and non-verbal participants. After the security of practising as a group, there is an opportunity for individual members to show what they remember and to express something personal in a short performance.

## Further development

1 The role of narrator can be passed to other group members.

2 A new sequence of mimes can be introduced around a different theme, such as getting caught in the rain.

# Puppets

7

# Finger puppets

These can be bought or easily made by cutting off the finger of a glove. Sew or stick onto the finger a selection of features to suggest a character: eyes, mouth, ears, hat, hair, arms. Make at least two of contrasting type: for example, an old one and a young one; a boy and a girl; a happy face and a sad face. A set of finger puppets might include different members and generations of a family, such as children, parents and grandparents, or different moods, such as happy, sad, cross and shy.

## Activity

The small size of these puppets makes them suitable for a sedentary group and for one-to-one work; they are also suitable for containing a lively group. The whole sequence can take place with the group sitting in a small circle.

The puppets are animated simply by moving the finger wearing the puppet in every direction possible. Index fingers or thumbs are usually the most flexible. The group leader introduces the first puppet to the group as a character, by name. She lets him take a bow, show himself off to his new acquaintances and make a short speech. She addresses the puppet with her usual voice, then models the use of an altered voice as part of the puppet's characterization. For example:

LEADER AS SELF: Hello, Grandfather Snow, welcome to our group.
LEADER AS GRANDFATHER SNOW: Thank you, I'm so pleased to be here, amongst such polite people. Very rare nowadays. Very different when I was young. . .

- Each participant has the opportunity to try on the puppet and either repeat the short performance as modelled or create their own variation.

The group leader introduces a second, contrasting puppet character in the same way. Again the group members take time to familiarize themselves with this puppet.

LEADER AS SELF: Welcome to our group, Boisterous Billy.
LEADER AS BOISTEROUS BILLY: Watcha, mate! Wanna game of football? Wanna fight? Wanna bit of trouble?

# Finger puppets

*continued from previous page*

- Introduce the idea that the two characters are going to meet each other. Two volunteers improvise the meeting and conversation. The group leader and other participants may help the encounter along by asking questions, always speaking to the puppet characters rather than the players. Other pairs may volunteer to continue the conversation or to stage a new meeting. Keep the puppets in a special place or container. At the end of the enactment the puppets are returned to their place in front of the whole group as part of a formalized de-roling.

## Further development

1 The group agrees on a title before each scene to build up a story: for example, making a date; having a quarrel; making up. The puppeteers have to follow the themes indicated in the title.

2 Introduce more puppets for a more complex scene involving the whole group, such as a family get-together.

PUPPETS

# Sock puppets

As with the finger puppets, sock puppets can be used informally by a sedentary group in a circle. It is also possible to present them theatrically from behind a table or screen, so that only the socked hand is visible. Sock puppets are easily made by drawing simple, strong facial features onto a sock with a marker pen. The sock fits over the entire hand and the face is animated by alternately stretching and screwing up the hand. These puppets are accessible to those without fine motor control. Make at least two contrasting types, such as one with a big, open mouth and small eyes, and one with wide-open eyes and a small mouth. (Features can also be sewn or stuck on, or painted with fabric paints.)

## Activity

Introduce each puppet to the group in character according to their strongest feature. For example:

Puppet with wide mouth: (loud voice) Hi, my name's Shouter. I've got lots to shout about. I'm the greatest, I'm the strongest, I'm the biggest and the bestest. Are you listening to me?

Puppet with wide eyes: (high voice) Oh! My, my! Fancy that! I didn't see you there. What's your name? My name's Surprise! Everything's a surprise to me. Oh, what's that?

Once the characters are broadly established, everyone in the group can try on the puppets for themselves, keeping the characteristic voice and personality traits of each and interacting with group members or with the other puppet character.

## Further development

1 Make further sock puppets in the group, such as Sad Sam, Happy Hal, Laughing Leila. What facial expressions are needed to convey these types?

2 Bring together different pairs of puppets for short improvised interactions in character.

3 Develop a simple character song for each puppet, such as the Sad Sam Blues.

4 Set up a television-style panel interview in which each puppet character is interviewed in turn, with interjections from other puppet panel members.

PUPPETS 7

# Vegetable puppets

Vegetable puppets can be made relatively easily in the group. Use odd-shaped potatoes, carrots, parsnips and turnips for the heads. Features can be drawn, pinned or stuck on to emphasize the characteristics suggested by the vegetable shapes. Make a hollow for the index finger to reach inside the head, and drape a cloth around the hand for the body. Thumb and third finger or little finger are used for the arms.

## Activity

As a group, create a royal vegetable court, with a selection of characters such as king, queen, prince, princess, jester, servants, guards, lords and ladies. Volunteers choose a puppet character and improvise short scenes. For example, the king and queen order breakfast in their rooms, which is brought by the servants; the princess tells her parents she wants to find a husband; a great ball is prepared, where lords and ladies are invited, food is served, the jester entertains the guests, and everybody dances; the princess chooses her bridegroom.

## Further development

Create a rustic community with vegetable puppets, including farmer, farmer's wife, children and various animals. In the case of the animals the vegetable can be used to represent both head and body. Instead of the cloth to hide the puppeteer's hand simply move the animals as necessary. Try to use mainly natural objects for the features, such as twigs, leaves, seeds and small stones, and natural coloured cloths for the bodies. Make a back-drop of a country scene, by painting an appropriate picture on card or a stretched cloth, or using a collage of pictures out of magazines. Let two or three at a time improvise various vegetable puppet encounters on the farm.

# Hand puppets

Hand puppets fit on the hand, sometimes extending up the arm. There is a wide selection available in the shops, representing animals and people. They come in different sizes, to fit child or adult hands. Some are easier to use than others; those with a small opening to a head and distinct arms demand considerable dexterity and can be very expressive, but may be less attractive at a tactile level.

Hand puppets can be used informally with the group sitting in a circle or moving freely in the drama space; semi-formally by bringing two chairs forward onto a stage area for two puppeteers and puppets, who create an improvised mini-performance for the group; and formally by working the puppets behind a table or screen as a stage, with the puppeteers invisible.

## Activity

A story can be used to provide the context for the puppets and to stimulate the imagination. For example, in the case of crocodile and snake puppets, the group leader begins to tell a story about the jungle. Some props suggestive of the jungle environment are set up and appropriate music or sound effects are created before the puppets are introduced. As the puppet characters are introduced, group members volunteer to manipulate the puppets and give them voices. The story develops as a group improvisation. The group leader takes on the role of narrator, drawing on the ideas of group members and helping to keep the group focused. Sound effects and other relevant characters are created through improvisation by the rest of the group. The puppets may be passed on to different puppeteers during the story, or may stay with one set of puppeteers until the story is over. In this case, other group members may be offered the puppets to create a new story or to repeat the original story in their own way.

For an improvised performance in pairs, set up two chairs facing the group and lay the two puppets on them. Invite volunteers to animate the puppets and to show the group what these two characters have to say to each other today. The group is invited to applaud after each short performance. Puppets and puppeteers take a bow. The puppeteers leave the puppets on the chairs for the next pair to come.

# Hand puppets

*continued from previous page*

In a third alternative, the group as a whole sets up a table, screen or puppet stage which enables puppets to be seen and heard by the audience while the puppeteers are invisible. Give puppeteer participants plenty of opportunity to swap places with someone in the audience group to explore the effect of their invisible work from the other side. Devise and rehearse a simple scene. Perform it within the group or to a wider audience. (See *Chapter 11*, on performance.) Sound effects and music can be rehearsed for live accompaniment or pre-recorded by the group.

## Further development

Take photographs of the various scenes of a rehearsed puppet play. Make an illustrated story book or animated film as a souvenir for the group.

PUPPETS

# Silhouette card puppets

These puppets are essentially two-dimensional and can be mounted on a three-dimensional base to stand alone or can be attached to a stick to be supported by a puppeteer. The group leader can prepare the puppets in advance, or allow time in the group for making them together. These puppets are relatively immobile, and are well suited to clear character types and known stories. (See *Chapters 9* and *10,* on dramatization and fairy tales/myths.)

## Activity: Snow White

Make the following out of firm card, using clear, bold features: Good Queen, Wicked stepmother, Beautiful Snow White, Handsome Prince, the seven dwarves, as one unit, the magic mirror, the cottage in the wood, and a transparent coffin (use transparent plastic sheet inside a cardboard frame). Help the group to remember the story and summarize it in simplified form, as follows.

Once upon a time there was a good queen, who was sewing at her open window and looking at the snow outside. She pricked her finger and, seeing the blood fall on the snow, she wished for a beautiful daughter, with red lips, fair skin and black hair. Her wish came true and Snow White was born, but the queen died and the king married again, a wicked and conceited woman who became Snow White's stepmother. Every day she would stand before her magic mirror and ask: "Mirror, mirror on the wall, who is the fairest of them all?" The mirror always told her that she was and that made her even more proud. One day, when Snow White had begun to grow up, the mirror told her that Snow White was now the fairest of them all. The queen was furious and threw Snow White out of the palace, to be eaten by bears in the forest.

Snow White wandered alone in the forest amongst the strange sounds and wild animals until she found a little cottage. She was so relieved that she went inside. No-one was there, so she made herself comfortable, had something to eat and lay down to sleep. What a shock it was for the seven dwarves to find her there when they came home to their cottage from working in the mines! What a shock for Snow White to wake up to find seven dwarves staring at her! But they soon made friends and the dwarves let her live with them, and begged her to be careful as her stepmother might come to find her.

# Silhouette card puppets

*continued from previous page*

One day, indeed, the wicked stepmother came to the cottage disguised as an old woman, and persuaded Snow White to eat a poisoned apple, so that Snow White would die, and she would be the fairest in the land again. Snow White took one bite of the apple and fell to the floor, dead. When the dwarves came home they tried to wake her, but could do nothing. They were so unhappy to lose their friend that they refused to bury her. Instead, they put her in a glass coffin where they could still admire her beauty.

One day a prince came by, saw the coffin and fell in love with Snow White immediately. He had never seen such a beautiful young woman before. He begged the dwarves to let him take the glass coffin to his palace so he could be near her. The dwarves could see he was in love with their friend, and agreed to let him take the glass coffin. As he took it, the coffin was jolted, and the piece of poisoned apple was knocked out of Snow White's mouth. She awoke, and fell in love with the prince. They went to his palace to be married immediately.

That day, when the wicked queen asked her mirror who was the fairest of them all, it replied, "Snow White, the prince's bride." She was beside herself with rage and envy, but everyone else in the land shared the happiness of Snow White and the prince, who lived happily ever after.

Having reminded the group of the story, let group members choose their puppet. They are responsible for moving the puppet in the relevant scenes and speaking for their puppet when there is dialogue. The group leader acts as narrator, if necessary, introducing each scene with guidelines for the puppeteers, such as "Let's see the wicked queen now and hear what she is asking her mirror."

## Further development

1 In a larger group, form a small musical orchestra, who set the atmosphere musically at the beginning and end of the piece. Try playing particular instruments during the performance to set the mood for different characters; for example, the sound of maracas every time the wicked queen makes an entrance.

# Silhouette card puppets

**2** If the group is comfortable with the idea, invite a small audience to see the show.

**3** Most fairy tales contain within them numerous stereotypes and cultural norms that are open to questioning. The group may alter the story in any way it chooses to make it more inclusive. Facilitators may help by giving various options for the group's new version of the story.

# Rod and stick puppets

Some people with learning difficulties are averse to putting their hand inside a puppet. This may be due to the physical sensation of constriction or a fear of merging with, being swallowed or overwhelmed by the puppet as the user's hand disappears. Rod and stick puppets are especially suitable for these people, provided they are able to grip the rods or can be given one-to-one assistance.

At the simplest level, stick puppets can be made by fixing a foam ball over the end of a short piece of doweling. The ball forms a head, which can be given features to denote a specific character, such as a clown, and specific facial expressions. The same principle of a soft toy on a stick is behind a variety of stick puppets on the market. In more sophisticated rod puppets, the puppet's limbs are controlled externally by means of an attached rod. These puppets can be manipulated by two or more people at once.

## Activity

In the group, create two life-size rod puppets, such as Fred Astaire and Ginger Rogers (or dancing partners from a current series of Strictly Come Dancing), each to be operated by two or three puppeteers. Use metal coat hangers and doweling to create shoulders and backbone, and to attach a head. Dress the male character in a suit, the female in a long-sleeved evening dress. Heads can be constructed from stuffed Lycra. Features can be stuck or sewn on, or represented in a stylized way through a mask. Finish the head with a hat or head-dress, and the arms with gloves, lightly stuffed. Attach rods for manipulating the puppets to wrists, shoulders and knees.

In small teams, practise working co-operatively to create basic movements; how does each character walk, wave, move from **A** to **B** or dance? Then bring the two puppets together and work on a sequence of activity. For example, they greet each other with a bow and a curtsey, dance together as music plays, go for a moonlit stroll, and he kneels to make a proposal of marriage. The group decides how the scene ends.

# Rod and stick puppets

## Further development

Create further large-scale, multiply-operated rod puppets as a group project. Start with an idea of a character, assemble a variety of materials and work out the requirements for the character together in the group. Attach rods for manipulating limbs and parts. Some suggestions: an octopus, a snail with mobile antennae and the ability to retreat into its shell; a mobile monkey with flexible legs and tail; fantasy creatures from outer space. Having made the puppets, group members explore freely what the puppets can do individually and together. This forms the basis for a story and performance, either within the group or to a small audience (see *Chapter 11*, on performance).

PUPPETS 7

Anna Chesner (2020), *Creative Drama Groupwork for People with Learning Difficulties*, Routledge

# Whole group dragon puppet

The giant dragon puppet is familiar to many from Chinese New Year celebrations. Making and moving a dragon as a whole group project can be fun and give a creative drama group a sense of bonding. The dragon is an expression of the whole group's creativity.

## Activity

Try using hula hoops as the skeleton, held together by coloured cloths, with streamers of cloth and paper. The hoops also form the framework for attaching rods, so that the dragon can be held and manipulated from underneath and the sides. Use a further hoop for the head of the dragon, with fabric stretched across it, and with features painted, stuck or sewn on. Small bells along the body of the dragon add a final touch and ensure that it will be heard as well as seen.

Everyone holds one or two rods to mobilize the dragon. Practise moving forward together, turning the dragon in a wide circle, getting it to undulate up and down and sway from side to side. If possible, organize a procession beyond the creative drama room. Those who do not wish to hold the dragon can go ahead or behind, providing musical accompaniment with tambourines, cymbals and maracas.

## Further development

1 In a large enough group, create two contrasting dragons and choreograph a dragon dance or dragon fight.

2 Film the procession/dance so that participants have a record of the event, and the opportunity to see themselves and their creation from the outside.

# CHAPTER 8

# Improvisation

# Improvisation preparation exercise:
## Follow and change

### Preparation

Take the group through a physical warm-up (see *Chapter 2*, on body work).

### Activity

Starting from a standing position in front of the whole group, one person performs a simple movement that they repeat with a steady rhythm until everyone has picked it up and the group is performing it in unison. This first leader chooses another group member with whom she changes places. The original movement continues throughout this transition and for a little while with the new leader. The new leader then introduces a new movement, ideally one which flows naturally from the first movement. The group again picks up this movement and the process continues until everyone has had an opportunity to lead.

As the exercise becomes familiar with practice, there should be a continuous flow. Each movement idea is continued until the new movement is introduced. The group leader may help the group keep in touch with the rhythm by using her voice to add emphasis to the movement. She may also need to remind the group who is the leader at any time and to encourage concentration on that person.

### Purpose

Satisfying improvisation depends on a group being able to support ideas which emerge from the group and to transform and develop an idea before the improvisation stagnates. This preparatory exercise works with both these skills within the framework of movement. The principle is one of "yes, and…"; in other words I accept and say yes to your offer, and I also have an offer of my own.

### Further development

1 The group tries to remember the sequence of movements and puts them together into a 'movement poem' in which each movement is performed in turn in a fluid sequence in unison by the group.

I M P R O V I S A T I O N

# Improvisation preparation exercise:
## *Follow and change* continued from previous page

**2** Try a similar exercise in pairs. *A* begins a movement and continues it while *B* picks it up. They continue for a while until *B* transforms it into a new movement and *A* picks this up, and so on.

CREATIVE DRAMA GROUPWORK FOR PEOPLE WITH LEARNING DIFFICULTIES

# Improvisation preparation exercise:
## *Mood change*

### Preparation

Put together a musical compilation, beginning with a slow, spacy (meditative and expansive) phase, then moving on to something staccato and punchy, and finally to something light and playful.

### Activity

The group leader talks through and models each phase. Group members join in as soon as they can, helped by the music. As the first music plays, they imagine themselves on the moon, almost weightless. Arms and legs float upwards and their movements are slow, flowing and big. Only the weight of the boots ensures that their feet are pulled down to the ground. All movements are slow and smooth.

When the music stops, they stand still for a moment, letting go of the image of the moon. The next piece of music is for fighting to. They imagine they are a great fighter, perhaps a boxer, a karate expert or a fighting animal. Listening to the rhythm of the music, they fight their imaginary opponent, using short, sharp, kicking, punching and scratching movements, without any actual physical contact with others. When the music stops, they stand still and let go of the image of their opponent. The final piece of music is light and airy. They imagine they are a string puppet and that their strings are being pulled. They move freely and lightly, without effort, and in any direction; they let themselves be taken by surprise. When the music stops, they shake out their bodies and roles, gently, and breathe.

### Purpose

This sequence gives practice in expressing roles physically and in responding to changes of mood.

### Further development

In a subsequent session, encourage interaction in the three states. On the moon, group members try to communicate with each other through their

IMPROVISATION 8

# Improvisation preparation exercise:
## *Mood change* continued from previous page

space suit, by pointing and mouthing. In the fighting sequence, they choose an opponent and fight, but without any physical contact. In the marionette sequence puppets can dance lightly together. When their puppeteer moves them on they change dancing partners quite suddenly.

# Improvisation preparation exercise:
## *Building a character*

### Preparation

The exercise works best with an assistant or co-leader. This person takes on the role of an actor in search of a character. A selection of cloths, hats and props is helpful.

### Activity

The group leader introduces the actor and explains his dilemma: he is an actor, but does not know what kind of role to play. The group's task is to give him some suggestions, initially in response to the group leader's questions, such as the following:

- Is this a man or a woman, or a creature?

- How old are they?

- What are they called?

- Where does this person come from? Somewhere near or far away? What is it like there?

- Where do they live now?

- What do they do?

- What do they like to eat and drink?

- Have they got a family?

- What do they wish for most?

- What are they afraid of?

As the questions are answered, the actor feels his way into the role, changing his posture and facial expression as required, finding a new voice perhaps and gradually acquiring pieces of costume and props as appropriate to the character. Once the character is broadly established, the group listens and watches as their creation 'comes to life', talking and moving around the space, fleshing out its story. They may ask questions or engage in other interactions with the character. Finally, the group leader chooses a moment for saying good-bye to the character and the group watches as the actor puts

# Improvisation preparation exercise:
## *Building a character* continued from previous page

away the props and pieces of costume. The group welcome him back into his own role, and talk about how they found the work.

## Purpose

This structure allows the group to build a dramatic character co-operatively and collectively. The actor models the process of taking on and taking off a make-believe role. Participants may relate to him from their everyday roles, or may naturally move in and out of make-believe roles themselves.

## Further development

1 The character created and its world can be used as the starting point for further work involving the whole group in a subsequent session. Group members may take on roles suggested by the character's story, such as people in the character's family, community or history.

2 The group creates a story about the character. Group members take on roles from the story and choose pieces of costume and props as appropriate. The story is told by means of a series of photographs, for which the group pose in role, creating a storyboard.

# Babble improvisation

## Preparation

Lead a face warm-up in a circle, everyone stretching their faces in all directions, paying particular attention to the mouth. Start babbling together in nonsense language, being as expressive as possible, making all sorts of sounds and backing them up with gestures and movements. Encourage free and spontaneous sounds.

## Activity

Everyone walks through the room, continuing to talk in nonsense language, as if very angry. Volume, facial expression and gesticulation can all be used. After a while, change the mood. The group continue babbling, but with a feeling of extreme sadness. Wailing and crying sounds may also be used, and body language that arises naturally from a feeling of sadness.

The mood changes again. This time group members imagine that they are in love and feel that they are walking on air. They continue babbling as if dreaming of their loved one, or talking to them. Finally, the mood changes to joy, with feelings of intense delight. Something has happened that makes them feel really good. Again, body language and babbling are used to convey the feeling.

## Purpose

The exercise focuses on expressive use of the voice without the pressure of finding words. It facilitates a playful exploration of the way feelings are conveyed through intonation and volume, enhanced by facial expression and gesture. It may help develop social awareness, empathy and learning to modulate and adapt to another person.

## Further development

Create a stage area with two chairs. Invite any two group members to come out and improvise a conversation in babble language. It can be an argument, a declaration of love, or may include a variety of different feelings. It is important that each player 'listens' to the other, and responds to their feelings. Afterwards the audience name the feelings they recognized and say what they imagined the scene was about.

# Building a machine

## Preparation

Spend some time in the group looking at pictures of a variety of machines, both simple and complex, such as a car, a stapler, a computer, a camera and a food processor. How do the different parts move? What does the machine as a whole do?

## Activity

The group chooses one of the machines already considered and recreates it dramatically, using body and voice. One person begins by performing a movement and sound suggested by one part of the machine, such as the wheel of a car. As he repeats this movement, the rest of the group joins in one at a time, each person adding a new movement and sound until the machine is complete: other wheels, ignition, windscreen wipers and so on.

## Purpose

The improvisation works on observation, imagination and co-operation. It promotes awareness of self in relation to others.

## Further development

1 Build a fantasy machine, using the same technique. Decide on its function before or after it is finished, e.g., a doughnut-making machine, a sausage-making machine, a machine that makes the weather.

2 Invent a story about the machine, as a group. The group leader may ask questions as necessary, such as

- "Where is the machine?",

- "Who uses it?" and

- "Does it always work well, and if not, what kind of problems does it have?"

# Where could we be?

## Preparation

Make sure there are plenty of things available in the space that could help the group to create an environment. Everyday and unusual objects, coloured cloths and musical instruments can all be used.

## Activity

Introduce the group to the idea of creating a place together in the drama room. It can be anywhere in the world, or beyond. To choose the place, you could start to gather ideas from participants, asking them to call out the names of the different countries they have heard of, and then ask the group to decide which one they would like to visit today in the drama. Alternatively, you could remind the group of where they are now and invite requests for other locations: "We are here in . . . in the middle of the town/country . . . on a wet/dry kind of day. If you had a wish, and as a group we could all go somewhere completely different for a little while, what kind of place would be interesting to visit?" Elicit suggestions and encourage the group to look at the alternatives and reach a consensus. Once the place has been agreed on, arrange the room so that there is a clear distinction between the empty acting area and the audience part of the room. Group members then build up the chosen environment using objects and cloths to represent all the important elements of the place.

From the audience part of the room, look at the space that has been created. Each person then goes into the space and takes on the role of a part of the scene they have built, such as the sun, the sea, or a palm tree in a tropical scene; an old car, motorbike or traffic light in a busy street scene; or a star, spaceship and astronaut in an outer space scene. The group leader interviews or visits each person in role, letting them introduce themselves to the group by showing how they move in role, what sounds they make and what they do in the scene.

With the setting and all the roles in the scene established, the improvisation is allowed to run freely, with each person playing their role in their own way. The group leader remains outside the improvisation and helps it to come to an end at an appropriate point. Possible ways of doing this include:

# Where could we be?

*continued from previous page*

**(a)** giving the group two minutes' notice to find an ending;

**(b)** calling "Freeze!", which means everyone holds their position as if the image were caught in a photo; then they 'unfreeze', coming out of the acting area, out of the role, into the 'here and now' part of the room; and

**(c)** announcing that night is falling, if possible dimming the light at the same time. Everything becomes still; after a few moments group members are asked to leave the action area and return to their own roles in the 'here and now' part of the room.

To de-role after the improvisation, the group leader and group members tell the story of the enactment. This creates some distance from the story. Before the end of the session, a name game or song is used to make sure that group members are clearly in the here and now. (See *Chapters 12* and *13,* on de-roling and closures.)

## Further development

1 Use the same structure on several occasions so that the process becomes familiar, while the content of the improvisation differs each time.

2 Set the stage in the same way. Then half the group take on key roles relating to the location, while the other half enter the scene as travellers, interacting with each other and the location freely.

# Travellers

## Preparation

Make sure that there is a variety of props and costumes close at hand that can be used as and when needed.

## Activity

The group leader introduces the idea that the group is going on a dramatic journey. The group will decide where they will go and how they will get there. First, gather ideas from the group about different possible modes of transport, such as walking, car, bus, tram, tube, train, bike, camel, horse, aeroplane, glider, barge, rowing boat, ship or submarine. Choose the mode of transport by consensus or by voting. This can be done sociometrically, i.e., a cloth or picture is used to represent each option, and distributed in the space. Each person moves towards the option that appeals to them, and the total votes are counted, the majority being the choice of the group. (This voting with the feet technique can be used in many contexts). The next task is to choose a destination, often suggested by the mode of transport: if the group are travelling by camel, they are likely to be in a desert, perhaps heading for an oasis; a rowing boat is likely to be used on a river or lake, perhaps to reach a favourite fishing spot or secluded picnic site.

The improvisation is contained within three main scenes: travelling there, being there and travelling back. The locations are prepared in advance by the group. The action begins when everyone is ready to travel. Group members may keep their own everyday roles, or take on other roles as required, such as the pilot and air hostess on a plane, a wandering nomad in the desert, or the loutish owner of a motorboat. Each time a role is assumed, participants can take a different hat or piece of costume, and put these aside when they leave the role. The group leader may also move in and out of role, sometimes moving the improvisation along by taking on a role within the drama, sometimes giving a group member confidence by accompanying them as a double in a role, sometimes standing apart from the drama and clarifying the action as narrator. The group leader is also responsible for time boundaries, making sure there is enough time for the return journey, and some time afterwards to reflect on the improvisation and come back to the here and now.

# Travellers

*continued from previous page*

## Further development

1 Return to the same place in a subsequent improvisation, by the same or a different method of transport. The group packs some useful things into a bag or case before leaving. How has the place changed? They write a postcard, or make a phone call, take a selfie, send an email home together.

2 Introduce a problem in the transport system. For example, the boat has sprung a leak. Will the passengers swim to shore, or is there someone on board who could fix it?

IMPROVISATION

# Magic carpet tour

## Preparation

As well as the usual range of props available, bring a very distinctive blanket or rug, large enough for the whole group to get onto. This will be the magic carpet.

## Activity

Introduce the group to the magic carpet and explain how it works: whenever the group is on it and holds hands it is capable of flying. Sometimes flying slowly, sometimes fast, it can go high or low. It can go anywhere and is particularly good at going to places people would love to be. As riders of the carpet, the group will see all sorts of places from above and, whenever they like, they can ask the carpet to take them down for a while. When they are ready to leave they just get back on the carpet again and hold hands so that they can fly on further. Eventually, they will come back to their starting point.

The group is invited to assume the take-off position, holding hands on the carpet. Group members create the sensation of flying through appropriate movement, and by making the whistling sounds of the wind. The group leader may make a commentary to enhance the make-believe quality for the group. Once 'airborne', invite participants to point down to what they can see below; if possible, pay a visit to each person's dream place. This may be an actual location, such as a snow-capped mountain, or a particular feeling, such as comfort. In each case, the group builds the essentials of the location simply and spends some time there, before moving on. Eventually, they return to base, roll up the carpet and spend some time talking about what happened on the journey.

## Further development

1 Invite the group to design and decorate its own magic carpet, for example by using fabric paints on a large piece of cloth. This becomes a stable prop for the group, used for travelling to a variety of make-believe destinations for improvisation work over a number of sessions.

2 Talk about dreams and wishes, those that have come true and those that have not.

# Place pictures

## Preparation

Bring to the group a variety of pictures with distinct locations. These are best collected over a period of time from magazines, postcards and the internet and can be mounted on card or laminated for ease of handling and longer use. Include a variety of indoor and outdoor locations, such as kitchen, living room, bar, restaurant or dance hall and mountain, bicycle track, busy street, harbour, beach, jungle or forest.

## Activity

The group leader shows three or four pictures to the group. She asks the group members what they see in each picture, then asks them to vote for the picture that interests them most at the moment. They can vote by raising a hand, or the group leader can lay out each picture and invite people to put a finger on the picture or stand by the one they are choosing.

Make a distinction between the acting area and the part of the room that does not represent an imaginary world. The group builds the picture in three dimensions in the acting area, then views it from outside. Who might live or be in such a space? Characters are introduced one by one into the acting area, with an appropriate prop or piece of costume. They have the opportunity to interact with each other freely within the make-believe environment. Finish the improvisation by giving the actors some minutes to come to a closure. Alternatively, ask them to 'freeze' at a dramatic point and take a real or imaginary photograph. As they step out of the photograph, they leave their fictional role. Allow time to retell the story, perhaps with reference to the original picture.

## Further development

Return to the place, the characters or the story and continue the improvisation over one or more further sessions. The story could become a long-running soap opera or improvised epic.

IMPROVISATION 8

# People pictures

## Preparation

Bring a variety of pictures of people to the group. A collection can be built up over time from magazines, postcards and the internet. Include a good cross-section in terms of age, race, gender and occupation; have single portraits as well as people in interaction.

## Activity

Give the group some time to examine three or four pictures and to discuss what they notice. Pass each picture around the circle and build up information gradually about each one. The group then chooses one character as the basis for a drama. One person takes on the role of the chosen character, with the relevant props and pieces of costume, such as a smiling older woman in a headscarf, holding a basket of freshly laid eggs. The character can be played by a male or female member of the group.

This person enters the acting area. Group members decide where the old lady might be and who might be with her; for example, she is selling her eggs in a market. Elements of the setting and other characters are brought on to the stage as appropriate: customers, other market vendors, perhaps a pickpocket. The scene is built up gradually, new characters entering the acting area one or two at a time, so that participants are aware of the whole as well as their own part in it. The improvisation then runs freely. It may reach a natural conclusion, or the group leader may suggest a reason congruent with the make-believe world for it to come to an end. For example, it is time for the market to close down for the evening, for the vendors to pack up and count their money, and for the customers to go on home with their shopping.

Allow time to remove pieces of costume, to put props and setting to one side, and to reflect on the work. The group may piece together the story from moments that each person remembers, and then give it a title.

## Further development

Choose two characters from the pictures at the outset. The group decides on a possible context for an encounter between the two, and the other roles are allocated accordingly.

# Characters from costume

## Preparation

An array of hats, scarves and other pieces of costume of various styles is put on display. It is helpful to have access to a full-length or large mirror.

## Activity

The group leader introduces the idea of creating a role from a piece of costume. She may demonstrate how, by putting on a certain hat, she can walk and talk differently and give herself a different name and personality for a little while, until she takes off the costume and returns to her usual role. Everyone chooses their own costume, puts it on and has a look in the mirror.

The group leader interviews each person and helps them establish their new role. How does this character walk? What is her name? What kind of work does she do? The group may decide together where such a group of people might be, for example, in a pub, at a bus stop or at a wedding. The space is prepared, the characters enter and interact freely in role. Try to bring the improvisation to a close in a way that fits the make-believe situation. For example, the pub is closing for the night, the bus arrives or the wedding couple leave for their honeymoon and the guests wave them on their way.

Allow time after the improvisation for letting go of the roles, removing costumes and set, and discussing the scene together. What was it like taking on the role of a different person for a while?

## Further development

Once the scene is in progress, the group leader calls "Freeze!" and briefly interviews each character in role from within the situation. What are you doing at the moment? How do you feel here? What do you think of what is happening around you? On the command, "Action!" the scene continues as before.

# Characters and situation from props

## Preparation

An array of objects is laid out on a table. These can be everyday objects such as a cup and saucer, cheese grater and umbrella. Include some less familiar ones, such as an old carved wooden box, a crown and something whose function is unclear. Allow at least one prop per group member.

## Activity

Allow some time for simply handling and exploring the objects. Everyone chooses an object and uses it as the basis for deciding who their character is. Pieces of costume may be added accordingly; for example, a telescope may lead to the choice of a ship's captain's hat.

The group leader helps the group come to an agreement about where the action starts. There may be more than one scene to the story, so not everyone needs to be in each scene, and there may be two or more locations for action in use simultaneously; for instance, some characters are on the ship, others are on the shore or in an aeroplane. At some point the story line should create a connection between the various characters and props; for example, the ship calls in to port, or plane crashes into the sea. The connection between the different sub-groups often happens spontaneously. If not, the group leader can guide the action from the role of narrator, or by taking on a catalyst role within the story for a while.

The group leader marks the end of the story from the role of narrator. Props and costumes are cleared away and the group returns to the here and now. They retell the story together as part of the de-roling process.

## Further development

Once the group has seen how the objects are used to create a story, ask each person to bring an object of their own that they would like to see used in an improvisation. This requires a level of trust in the group that objects will be treated with care within the improvisation.

# Improvised scenes from everyday life:

## *The cafe*

### Preparation

Create a stage area and an off-stage area.

### Activity

Set up groups of two or three chairs on the stage and introduce the title of a scene, such as 'The Cafe'. Invite group members to enter the scene and see what happens. Some may be customers and others waiters. Maybe they are at a table with someone they know, or maybe they are sitting with a complete stranger. Do they talk? Is the waiter friendly, efficient or forgetful?

Give the scene some time to run, then ask the group to freeze. Bring the focus to one area, in which action recommences while the others watch, so that everyone has a chance to hear what is happening there. Then move the focus to another area. If too little is happening spontaneously, the group leader can help the scene along by conducting interviews in role; for example: "So you and your wife are having a rest from the shopping? What have you been shopping for? Is it busy in town today? So how are you feeling now? Tell your wife, and we'll listen. . ."

### Further development

1  Use a similar approach with different known environments, such as a train carriage, a lift or club.

2  Suggest a rule that actors enter the stage area one or two at a time, and that the rest watch the scene develop until the next one or two make their entrance. These can take into account what has already happened.

IMPROVISATION 8

# Improvised scenes from everyday life:

## *A family get-together*

### Preparation

Introduce the idea that the group is going to improvise being one large family, including distant relations or close friends of the family. Everyone can choose the kind of role they want. This is an opportunity to try out a role that is unfamiliar, to find out what it is like to be a grandparent or to be the youngest child in the family instead of the oldest, or to be an adventurous aunt who is always travelling. Everyone says a few words about their role, such as "I am the grandmother, the mother's mother, and I am a quiet person who enjoys cooking." When all the characters have spoken, the group decides on where and why the family come together, perhaps for a birthday, a funeral, a meeting about a crisis, or because someone has won a lot of money.

### Activity

The group sets up the stage as a shared activity. Everyone takes one piece of costume and a prop to help them in the role, and finds their starting place on the set. One by one, everyone introduces themselves in role, to remind themselves and the group what role they are playing, and what they are called.

The group leader calls "Action!" and the scene unfolds freely. After some time she calls "Freeze!" and one by one the characters say how they are feeling or what they are doing. For example, "I am the baby here, and I like the way my brother is playing with me under the table." The improvisation continues for a while, with the instruction to bring it to an end. If the group has difficulty finding an ending, the group leader can introduce information from the outside, such as "The restaurant is closing, and everyone must go home." At the end everyone is told to freeze again and, after a countdown of three, to let go of the story and return to their own role in the group.

Remove items of costume and clear the set as part of the de-roling process, and make sure there is time to reflect and give feedback about the improvisation before closing the session. (See *Chapters 12* and *13*, on de-roling and closures.)

# 9

# Dramatization

# Dramatizing a known story:

## Noah's Ark

Stories from the religious traditions offer plenty of dramatic scope. Choose a story according to the time of year, the weather or the current interest of the group. This one might suit a rainy day. To begin with, the group familiarizes itself with the story. In later sessions some or all the key scenes are enacted as individual units.

### Preparation

Piece together in the group the story of Noah. These are the key elements of the story:

1 God is angry with his creation and decides to send a flood to wipe it out.

2 Noah is a good and very old man. He has a wife, three sons and three daughters-in-law.

3 God tells Noah to build an ark. He tells him exactly how to make it, with rooms for his family, and for two of every kind of animal and bird. There must be plenty of food on board as well. Noah builds the ark as instructed.

4 Seven days later the rain begins to fall. Noah leads his family on board the ark with pairs of all the creatures in creation.

5 They are safe, but the rains fall heavily for forty days and forty nights. All the earth disappears under water, even the highest mountains. They are the only ones who have survived, as the ark rises up and floats on the surface of the water.

6 Noah sends out a raven and a dove to fly over the water and find land. At first the birds can find no land, but then the dove finds an olive tree and brings back a leaf to Noah.

7 God sends wind to begin to dry out the water. Gradually, the waters sink and the ark comes to rest on the top of Mount Ararat.

8 Eventually, God tells Noah to come out and let all the creatures out of the ark to begin their new life. Noah does this, and thanks God. God promises never to destroy his creation again.

# Dramatizing a known story:

*Noah's Ark* *continued from previous page*

## Activity

Enact the story, scene by scene, over several sessions. Involve the whole group in building the environment and taking on multiple roles, as in the following suggestions.

**Scene 1: God looks down** God needs a high position to look down on his creation, perhaps from on top of a table. He or she may have a staff as a symbol of their authority. The group decides what god sees as he looks down: flowers, trees, animals, people fighting? The whole group take up roles from the created world. One by one, those who want to can leave the scene, and make a role reversal as God. They take up their position as God, looking down on the earth and deciding to teach everyone a lesson. Those who do not want to play God alone can play a multiple God as a pair or small group. It is also possible for the whole group to play God together, looking down at an imaginary creation, saying and pointing to what they see.

**Scene 2: The good family** The group builds up their idea of a good family by showing Noah and his wife, the three children and their spouses. The numbers and relationships of the Noah family members can be adapted according to the wishes of the group. Group members volunteer for the character that interests them. Each character may be at work or play. What is each person doing? Improvise a prop, if appropriate, and one piece of costume. Find a mime for each person's activity. Show them all at once, then freeze as if for a photograph. In a larger group there may be several versions of the good family Noah.

**Scene 3: Building the ark** According to God's instructions, Noah and his family build the ark. The role of God in this scene may be that of a foreman who continually gives instructions and involves himself in the work; or he may give a set of plans and instructions at the beginning and then watch from afar while the humans get on with the work. Building the ark is a creative challenge for the whole group. They can look at a picture or model of the ark, then build it using mats, playshapes, cardboard boxes, polystyrene bricks, chairs, tables and cloths. Building tasks can be mimed as a group, with appropriate sound effects: chopping wood, hammering nails, painting, waterproofing, hanging the door.

# Dramatizing a known story:
## Noah's Ark

The ark should be large enough to contain the whole group while leaving enough room outside it for the procession of animals.

**Scene 4: Boarding the ark** This scene begins with the rain falling. The whole group creates the sound of the rain falling by tapping hands on thighs, shaking maracas or rainsticks or tapping canes on the floor, and making rain sounds with the mouth. The rain starts gently then builds in a crescendo, perhaps with thunderbolts on drum and gong.

The animals are led in pairs onto the ark. This requires some preparation. The whole group can explore as a warm-up game how different animals move and look. Anyone in the group may call out the name of an animal or bird and everyone then experiments with ways to represent it. Make sure that different physical levels are included, such as snake, mouse, ostrich and eagle. For the enactment, the group splits into pairs and each pair volunteers to represent a particular creature. Noah calls out for each animal in turn and one of his family leads the pair up a ramp or along a cloth into the ark. Once inside, the pairs can stay there in role as that animal or return outside to represent a different creature being led on board. Finally, Noah and his family board the ark and close the door.

**Scene 5: Life in the ark** As the rain falls outside and the waters rise, those in the ark are safe and warm. What do they do? Perhaps they tell stories about their life before the flood. Perhaps they squabble, or keep looking outside to see if the rain has stopped. Noah probably keeps count of the days and nights it has rained. Each person chooses an animal or human role and the group improvises the scene.

**Scene 6: Looking for land** The animals in the ark get impatient and homesick for dry land. In this episode the animals and people express their impatience and discontent in sounds and words. You might orchestrate a group moan at this point. Noah sends out a raven and a dove to search for land. These two roles can be taken by two group members, one with a white cloth, the other with a black one. The other animals watch from the ark as they circle over the water. The group inside the ark are first hopeful, then unhappy as the birds return without success. Maybe another pair of group members repeat the process. Then God sends a wind to dry the waters. This

# Dramatizing a known story:

## *Noah's Ark* *continued from previous page*

episode can be represented by God himself blowing from above onto the whole scene or with a second group member in role as the wind sent by God. The ark comes to rest on the top of a mountain, perhaps with a big bump that makes all in the ark jump. The scene ends hopefully when the dove brings back a leaf. There is land out there, and they are longing to find it again.

**Scene 7: Leaving the ark** God gives Noah permission to open the doors and let everyone out of the ark. The animals and people come out and begin to explore the new land, each in their own way. After months swaying on the water it is strange to walk on dry land. The group can explore this difference, swaying together in rhythm on the ark, then trying to move on dry land. At a certain moment, perhaps signalled by the sound of a drum or gong, everyone stops and witnesses the interchange between Noah and God. Noah gives thanks on behalf of all the creatures. God in turn gives a blessing for their new life. As in the first scene, everyone who wants to can take the role of either God or Noah in this interchange.

## Further development

1 The dramatization could form the basis of a performance piece. (See *Chapter 11*, on performance.)

2 Ask group members for a favourite moment from the story. Re-create each moment briefly, through a mime, a tableau or short action replay.

3 Discuss the variety of species in the story and the problem of climate change and endangered species today. Dramatize the interdependence of creatures and their environment.

4 Choose a story from another culture for contrast (such as an episode from the *Ramayana* or *Journey to the West*) using a similar approach.

# Dramatizing a poem:
## *There Was a Princess Long Ago*

This is a traditional children's rhyme, although thematically not without interest for adolescents and adults. It can be spoken or sung to a traditional tune.

### Preparation

Some simple props can be used to clarify roles and enhance the fairy-tale aspect of the poem:

> a cardboard crown or light-coloured veil for the princess, a dark shawl for the wicked fairy, and a stick to represent her wand, large green and brown cloths for the forest, and a crown and sword for the prince.

(Some recorded music may be used for a courtly celebration dance at the end.)

### Activity

Establish who will play the princess, the wicked fairy and the prince for the first round. The roles can be played by people of either sex. The poem is short enough to repeat with different group members playing different roles. The group leader recites the poem verse by verse. There is a lot of repetition, which helps group members to join in. Each verse is accompanied by actions.

> *There was a princess long ago, long ago, long ago.*
> *There was a princess long ago. Long, long ago.*

(The group stands in a circle. The princess puts on her crown or veil and steps into the centre of the circle. Everyone bows or curtseys to her and she nods or curtseys back.)

> *Now she lived in a big high tower, a big high tower, big high tower*
> *Now she lived in a big high tower. Long, long ago.*

# Dramatizing a poem:

## *There Was a Princess Long Ago* continued from previous page

(The group creates the tower. Holding hands, they stand on tiptoe and reach up as high as possible. The princess remains in the middle, and may look out of the different 'windows' created by the arms.)

> *A wicked fairy waved her wand, waved her wand, waved her wand.*
> *A wicked fairy waved her wand. Long, long ago.*

(One group member leaves the circle and fetches her wand and cloak. She returns and waves her wand at the princess, laughing wickedly.)

> *The princess slept for a hundred years, a hundred years, a hundred years.*
> *The princess slept for a hundred years. Long, long ago.*

(The princess lies down in the middle of the circle.)

> *A thick dark forest grew around, grew around, grew around.*
> *A thick dark forest grew around. Long, long ago.*

(All except the princess and the prince crouch down and begin to grow around her in a tangle of intertwined arms and legs. Dark cloths may be held between several people to create the sense of darkness. The prince waits to one side.)

> *A handsome prince came riding by, riding by, riding by.*
> *A handsome prince came riding by. Long, long ago.*

(The prince with his sword and crown gallops around the outside of the forest; then takes his sword and, without hurting anyone, forces his way through the dense trees.)

> *He kissed her hand to wake her up, wake her up, wake her up.*
> *He kissed her hand to wake her up. Long, long ago.*

(The prince kneels by the princess, takes her hand and kisses it. The princess wakes up, rubs her eyes and lets the prince help her to stand up.)

> *So everybody's happy now, happy now, happy now.*
> *So everybody's happy now. We're happy now.*

# Dramatizing a poem:
## *There Was a Princess Long Ago*

(Everybody claps or waves their hands. The celebration can be extended by playing a piece of recorded music and dancing together in honour of the royal marriage.)

### Further development

1 Read and dramatize the fuller Grimm's version of the story of *Sleeping Beauty*.

2 Make pictures of fairy-tale princesses and princes. Think about modern versions of these fairy-tale figures. Inspired by the traditional story, the group can make a modern love story.

DRAMATIZATION 9

# Dramatizing a song:
## My Bonnie Lies Over the Ocean

All kinds of songs can be used as the basis for a drama. This is a traditional song with an easy melody and plenty of repetition. It lends itself easily to adaptation.

### Preparation

Sing the traditional version of the song together:

> *My Bonnie lies over the ocean*
> *My Bonnie lies over the sea*
> *My Bonnie lies over the ocean*
> *Oh bring back my Bonnie to me.*
> *Bring back, bring back,*
> *Oh bring back my Bonnie to me, to me.*
> *Bring back, bring back,*
> *Oh bring back my Bonnie to me!*

Instead of the hero of the song being Bonnie Prince Charlie, as originally intended, each group member will have the chance to be the hero or heroine of the song. At first they wait alone across the water, while the group row towards him in a boat and sing the song, substituting their name for Bonnie. By the end of the verse they reach their group member and bring them on board the boat. They are reunited.

### Activity

The group prepares the setting. Contrasting cloths can be used to represent the sea and the land. The boat can be created by group members sitting behind each other on the floor, legs apart on either side of the person in front. From this position they can mime a rowing action and slide forwards on their bottoms. If this position is physically too difficult, they can stand in the boat and shuffle forward as they row. For variety, each person can choose which country their piece of land represents and the boat journey can be correspondingly long or short. They may wave to the boat to help guide it towards them.

# Dramatizing a song:
## *My Bonnie Lies Over the Ocean*

### Purpose

This dramatization gives the group as a whole a challenge in moving co-operatively. At the same time, each individual has a defined period of time in which they are alone and the special person for the group.

### Further development

1 Talk about how it feels to be separated from someone loved, and how it feels to be reunited.

2 Continue the theme of boats by singing and moving to 'Michael, Row the Boat Ashore' or 'Row, Row, Row the Boat Gently down the Stream'.

DRAMATIZATION

# Scenes from films

Films or television programmes can provide a rich source of inspiration. A character or scene from a film that excited, moved or interested one group member can be recreated dramatically in the group as a way of sharing something of personal significance with the whole group.

## Preparation

Introduce the theme of favourite films and programmes. Ask the group to think of as many films as they can that have impressed them or soaps that they watch. Then ask each person to choose one moment or one character from a film and to describe it briefly.

## Activity

Each person's suggestion is recreated in the group, either briefly and all within one session or at more length and over a period of several sessions. The person whose scene is explored 'directs' the scene. The group leader helps the director focus on the precise moment or sequence of moments to be recreated in the group. Set up the starting moment as a still photo or tableau, using whatever props are around to recreate the atmosphere. The director may wish to play one of the roles herself and can choose or negotiate with other group members to play the other roles.

Beginning with the still photo, the director places each character in the scene and gives them a word or a gesture that captures the essence of their character at this moment in the action. The still photo can be followed by a short period of action, according to the guidelines of the director. If sound effects are needed, one or more participants can prepare and rehearse these before going into action. Finish with another freeze frame. The group leader invites each character to say one word about how they feel in the role.

If the director has played a role in the scene, let him return to the role of director at this point, by using a stand-in or empty chair to represent his position in the final photo. This allows the director to view the scene from outside. The group leader invites the director to give a title to the scene, to call "Cut!" and thank the actors. Before going on to another scene from another film, make sure everyone has de-roled: they may physically brush

# Scenes from films

themselves down and wipe away the old role, or make a statement about one way in which they are different from the character they played. (See *Chapter 12*, on de-roling.)

## Further development

1 When all the scenes have been presented, everyone is invited to return to their favourite role, with the help of props and costume. The group decides where this collection of people might meet: for instance, at a station, at a party, on a cruise ship or in a dream. The scene unfolds as an improvisation. How do these characters get on together? What do various pairs or groupings have in common? From time to time, the group leader asks the group to freeze and focus on the action of one sub-group.

2 Write a new film together as a group. Choose characters and a situation. Make a video or series of still photographs, which can be pasted into a story album.

DRAMATIZATION 9

# Dramatizing Shakespeare:

## *The Tempest*

Shakespeare's plays tend to have rather complicated plots and sub-plots. This does not exclude the possibility of working on a Shakespeare play within the context of a creative drama group for children or adults with learning difficulties. Indeed, such a group gives a wonderful opportunity for an introduction to Shakespeare. Rather than dramatizing the whole story, allow the group to focus on the central situation of a play, or the core conflict. There follows an approach to *The Tempest*. A similar approach can be used with other Shakespeare plays. (See also *Romeo and Juliet*, below.) Simply identify a core theme, summarize as much of the plot as is strictly necessary to appreciate the core theme, and devise one or two scenes to explore the theme dramatically.

### Preparation

Summarize the plot, as follows. The central situation of *The Tempest* is a magic island, full of strange spirits. Prospero rules over the island and is master of the island's magic. He has a daughter, Miranda, who is naive and innocent, and knows no human beings other than her father. Apart from Prospero and Miranda, there are many nature spirits on the island who are all under Prospero's command. His favourite is Ariel, who is fast and light. Ariel enjoys teasing Caliban, who is a monster, slow and heavy, the son of a witch, but in his own way charming and very much part of the atmosphere of the island.

### Activity

Having outlined the basic situation, create the island as a whole group activity, representing the sea, caves, forests and rivers. Make the island mysterious by hanging strips of cloth, veils and bells, where possible, and playing atmospheric background music (such as a combination of natural sounds and flute or bells).

Warm up to choosing roles by doing a brief sequence in which everyone gets to explore being Prospero, Miranda or spirits of the island. Then let group members choose a role. Prospero is old, wise and very powerful, able to command the spirits and make them move or 'freeze' with a word and a gesture. Miranda is pretty, kind and interested in the world around her. Ariel is playful and fast, and willing to serve Prospero faithfully. Caliban is

# Dramatizing Shakespeare:
## *The Tempest*

ugly, clumsy and rather sad. (This role may be played by a helper if group members are averse to adopting the role of the ugly outsider. Dramatically roles like this can be great fun to play). Other group members can take the role of nature spirits, inhabiting the air, rivers, trees and sea. Use costume and perhaps face paint to characterize the roles and let each person introduce themselves on the set in character. Where appropriate, the nature spirits each have a musical instrument to create sound effects.

The action can be very simple. Start by visiting the various nature spirits and seeing them in action. The sea spirits can create waves through movement, or through sending ripples through a large cloth. River spirits lie on their cloth rivers and make gurgling or rushing sounds. Wind and air spirits, led by Ariel, can run through the island, gently touching the trees, bells and hanging strips. The tree spirits can rustle their leaves, wave their branches and perhaps sing their own song. Miranda can go on a tour of the island, meeting the various spirits.

When the features and characters of the island are established, Prospero emerges from his cave, and starts exercising his power. He sends Ariel on errands, orders the nature spirits to go about their activities or to stop in their tracks (freeze). He makes the wind blow and the sea storm. Prospero sees the island as his own and enjoys his power. He waves his magic wand and the island obeys his wishes.

## Further development

1 Pass the role of Prospero on, so that several people have the chance to be in charge and exercise their magic.

2 Introduce the next part of the story: Prospero creates a storm and causes a ship to be wrecked on the island. Miranda meets her first humans and falls in love with Ferdinand. Explore the shipwrecked people's reactions to the magic island through improvisation, (See *Chapter 8*).

# Dramatizing Shakespeare:
## *Romeo and Juliet*

While the essence of *The Tempest* is best captured through the setting, in the case of *Romeo and Juliet* the essence of the play is in the conflict between the two families and the forbidden love between Romeo and Juliet.

## Preparation

Summarize the plot, as follows. There are two wealthy and powerful families in Verona, the Montagues and the Capulets. A long time ago there was a quarrel between the families and the feud has continued, so that now all Montagues are expected to hate all Capulets and vice versa. Even the servants of the families take part loyally in the feud.

## Activity

Having introduced the story of *Romeo and Juliet* as above, let the action begin.

**Scene 1** Let the group divide into two, and create the two families, including attendants. Amongst the Montagues is Romeo, young, handsome and gallant, amongst the Capulets is Juliet, young, beautiful and innocent. Other characters include friends, parents and servants.

Explore the conflict between the two sides, using the modern analogy of rival football club supporters. Let each group choose a slogan, such as "We are the Capulets and we're the best!" or "Montagues forever! Down with the Capulets!" The two sub-groups practise their slogans and chant them loudly, trying to drown out the other sub-group. Explore the tension further in movement. Members of each sub-group huddle together at either end of the room, as if at either end of a street. Each group must move to the other end of the room, staying huddled together. When passing the others, each side tries to show that they are not afraid and that they are better than the others. Try to create an atmosphere as if a fight could break out at any moment; it is only avoided by steering clear of the other group. If possible, the group leader and assistant join each huddle, directing the scene from within.

**Scene 2** The hostility of Scene 1 one is the background to the forbidden love affair between Romeo, a Montague, and Juliet, a Capulet. After the group focus of the first scene, the famous balcony scene provides an opportunity for different pairs in the group to enact a love scene. Romeo and Juliet

# Dramatizing Shakespeare:
## Romeo and Juliet

have met at a party and have fallen in love. After the party, Romeo finds out who Juliet is and where she lives. Begin as a group by setting the scene. There is a wall into the Capulets' orchard that Romeo must get over, and which symbolizes the risk he takes in going near Juliet at all. There is a balcony from Juliet's room, where she can stand and look down into the gardens. (Use a sturdy table to climb onto or some other way to indicate the difference in height.) It is night time, so there is also a moon shedding its light over the scene. Romeo climbs over the wall to be near Juliet and dream of her. Juliet comes onto the balcony and, believing herself to be alone, starts talking about Romeo: how she wishes he were not a Montague or she a Capulet, and how she would even give up being a Capulet to be with him. Romeo hears this, but remains hidden at first behind a tree. Then, convinced that she loves him, he shows himself and declares his love to Juliet.

Group members of either sex can play Romeo or Juliet. Some may be more comfortable playing female to female or male to male. It is a romantic scene, so encourage the actors to find romantic ways of declaring their love. Read out an excerpt from the Shakespeare text (Act 2, Scene 1) if the group is receptive, to suggest some of the imagery they can use. Someone may also take the role of the moon, casting a pale light on the scene and commenting on what she sees.

A simple piece of costume can be used to represent the roles, such as a white muslin dressing-gown for Juliet, a dashing cape over Romeo's shoulders, and a silver drape for the moon. Let as many couples as want to try out the scene, passing on the pieces of costume to transfer the role. At the end, allow time to de-role. Dismantle the set, remove pieces of costume and come together as a group to reflect on the story and the experience of acting the two scenes. (See *Chapter 12,* on de-roling.)

### Further development

1 Identify modern-day love stories from television soaps, current films, current affairs and so on. Make still tableaux of some of these couples, such as Superman and Lois Lane, Sandy and Danny from *Grease*, Latika and Jamal from *Slumdog Millionaire*, etc.

# Dramatizing Shakespeare:

## *Romeo and Juliet* continued from previous page

**2** What experience do group members have of belonging to a group and of conflict with other groups?

**3** Listen to the words of a current or well-known pop song dealing with the theme of love. Perhaps some of the imagery is similar to Shakespeare's (sun, moon, roses, sweetness, angels and so on).

# Current affairs:

## *Television interview*

Local, national or international news can be explored through creative drama. Group members may come to the group already warmed up to something read in a newspaper, heard on the radio, seen on television or overheard in a conversation. The drama can be used to express feelings or opinions about the news and to help understand the issues involved. The format of a television interview can help to highlight different perspectives on these issues.

### Preparation

Discuss the issue as a group. Pool information about the people involved.

### Activity

Set out a chair for each character or type of character to be interviewed, such as an expert, a politician, a local resident, someone directly affected, an eye witness. Group members volunteer for a role that interests them, adopt a suitable prop or piece of costume and sit in the appropriate chair. Those not on the panel take the role of the studio audience. The group leader is interviewer, going from person to person with a microphone. Questions and responses can also be taken from the audience. At the end of the programme, the interviewer summarizes the various positions. Where appropriate, the audience may be asked to express their opinion with a show of hands. The interviewer closes the programme formally.

Give plenty of time to de-role. Those who were in role on the panel can discuss whether they hold the same opinions personally as the characters they played. Did their understanding or perspective change through playing the role?

### Further development

Record a 'radio discussion programme' in which different opinions are expressed about an issue of current concern. The recording may run continually or be turned off while panellists prepare or rehearse their contribution. Listen to the recording.

DRAMATIZATION

# Dramatizing a personal story

The life experience of any group member can provide the material for a personal story enacted in the group. This story may be based on a past experience, a present situation or a future possibility. An important role for the group leader is to help give the enactment a clear focus and form.

## Preparation

Each group member checks into the group with a piece of current news, or an issue that they have been thinking about. This can be done as a verbal exercise or in combination with a mime. The group decides which story they would be interested in dramatizing, through discussion or a show of hands. Themes may vary, from the recent loss of an important personal possession, to an impending marriage in the family.

## Activity

The group leader helps to clarify briefly the important points of the story with the story teller, for the sake of the whole group who will be involved in the acting. The story is divided into a sequence of scenes. It may be appropriate to begin the story at an earlier point. For example, when structuring a series of scenes about the recent loss of a personal possession, it would be helpful to go back to the time when the possession was acquired, and a scene before it was lost, before showing the scene when its loss was discovered.

Group members may volunteer for roles, or be invited to play particular roles by the story teller. The story teller can choose to play her own or a different role in the story, or may prefer to watch the enactment as part of the audience. The group leader can act as narrator to help guide the flow of the action. At the end of the enactment of the story as originally told, the group leader may ask the story teller if she would like to add an extra fantasy scene as an ending. At the end of the enactment, all players remove props and pieces of costume belonging to the characters. The group comes together and chooses a title for the piece.

CREATIVE DRAMA GROUPWORK FOR PEOPLE WITH LEARNING DIFFICULTIES

# Dramatizing a personal story

## Further development

1 Once this way of working is familiar in the group, give each participant the opportunity to tell a personal story in the group over a series of sessions, using the same structured approach.

2 Invite different stories relating to a common theme, such as family, growing up, love, change.

DRAMATIZATION

# Dramatizing the history of the group

When a group of people have been together for a while, there is a sense of shared history. This applies to groups of people living together, working together or playing together, as in a creative drama group. It is interesting to take stock by dramatizing the shared story, particularly at a time of change or on a shared anniversary.

## Preparation

Introduce the subject of the history of the group and invite brief reminiscences from group members. Recollections may be both happy and unhappy, including new arrivals as well as losses and disruptions.

## Activity

The group leader introduces each scene in chronological order, starting at the beginning. The group builds a tableau of the people who were there at the beginning, those who are still present playing themselves, with a chair or other symbol to represent those who are no longer in the group. The group leader may also represent herself with a chair so that she can view the tableau from the outside. Participants adopt a position in relation to each other that represents their feelings and relationships at that time. Each person says one phrase or makes a gesture to describe their position in this scene.

Step by step, the group leader guides the group through a sequence of tableaux. A new phase arises with each change in the group composition, in external factors affecting the group or in internal conditions and relationships. Each phase is represented by a new tableau, and a new statement of feelings or relationships. Scenes of particular significance can be marked by giving them a title agreed on by the whole group. After the enactment, allow time for the group to come together and give feedback on the process. Which parts made them feel happy, sad, angry or hopeful?

## Further development

Ask each group member to build a tableau representing a hoped-for future phase in the group.

# Dramatization of a current group dynamic:

## *Group body*

The metaphor of the group as a body is used to help group members express indirectly how they see their place and function in the group.

### Preparation

A variety of cloths should be available to help different parts of the body differentiate their roles.

### Activity

The group leader introduces the idea of the group as a very large body made up of each group member. Group members choose parts of the body and place themselves spatially in relation to the other body parts. For example, one person plays the right hand, another the heart, another the eyes, and so on. The group discuss and negotiate where the different parts are. When each person has a place, they may use a cloth or prop to establish their role. They state what part of the body they are, and what they do as a body part, as follows: "I am the mouth, and I eat, drink and talk."

Once the roles are clear, the group leader gives the whole body a task to perform involving co-operation of all its body parts. This task may be as specific as walking from one side of the room to the other, or as extended as showing a whole day in the life of the body, from waking up in the morning to going to sleep again at night. When the enactment is over, but before the group body is dismantled, each body part makes a brief statement about how they feel in the body.

After de-roling, the group comes together in a circle and discusses the exercise. Which body part was most in control? Were any body parts overused or underused? If each group member had the chance to choose again, which part would they rather be?

# Dramatization of a current group dynamic:

## *Group body* continued from previous page

### Further development

Before de-roling, each body part makes a statement or request to another body part they had contact with in the enactment. They may wish to give thanks for support and good teamwork, or they may need to ask to be treated differently by the other body part.

# Dramatization of preferences and choices – sociometry

This structure is flexible and can be used whenever a choice is to be made or preferences are expressed in the group. These choices may relate to real life issues beyond the context of the creative drama group, as well as to internal issues to do with the direction of work in the group. The essence of the structure is the dramatic use of space.

## Preparation

Introduce the topic around which a choice is to made. For example, the group is going on holiday together: what kind of holiday would most interest them?

## Activity

Areas of the room are used to symbolize the different kinds of holiday available. A blue cloth may represent the seaside in one corner; a rope may be placed in another corner, representing an adventure activity holiday; puppets in a third corner may represent a trip to a Disney centre.

Before making any decisions, everyone is free to go to each area and talk about or mime what they would expect from such a holiday. They may also ask questions about an area they know less about. After considering the possibilities imaginatively, everyone goes to the area of their choice, i.e., they vote with their feet. The group leader counts the votes, announces the numbers and asks for a short statement from each person as to why they have made that particular choice.

More detailed choices can be made in a subsequent round. If a beach holiday has been chosen, there may be a choice between a one-week holiday abroad and a two-week holiday nearer home, in which case two areas would be set up and the procedure would be repeated as above.

## Further development

When more than one person has an idea for an enactment in the group, they give their idea a title and step forward. They literally stand up for that

# Dramatization of preferences and choices – sociometry

*continued from previous page*

idea. When all available options are represented, everyone votes for the idea that draws them most at that moment. The vote is made by placing a hand on the shoulder of the person standing for that idea. The weight of opinion is thus shown visibly and concretely and without relying heavily on discussion. The majority decision is followed after the group leader has thanked representatives of all the options for standing up for their idea.

CREATIVE DRAMA GROUPWORK FOR PEOPLE WITH LEARNING DIFFICULTIES

# 10

# Fairy tales and myths

# Introduction

There follow four fairy tales and a myth, and ideas for how to use them. Each example begins with a simplified narrative and is followed by suggestions for preparation and an overall approach to the work. The narrative is then broken down into sample scenes which may be taken as guidelines for enacting the story.

# The three wishes

## The narrative

Once upon a time there was a couple, who lived simply in their cottage. They were not rich, but they were not poor either. One winter's evening, they sat by the fire warming their hands and talking about their next-door neighbours, who had more money than they did.

The wife said, "I wish we were richer and had nice things." Her husband agreed. "Yes," he said, "If only there were fairies who granted wishes." No sooner had he said this than a beautiful fairy suddenly appeared in the room. "I am a fairy," she said, "and I will grant you three wishes. But be very careful what you wish for, because I will grant the first three wishes you make, and no more. Wish well!" She disappeared as suddenly as she had appeared.

"Oh, I can't wait to start wishing," said the wife, full of excitement. "There's all sorts of things I want." "No, let's wait until tomorrow," said her husband, who wanted to be sensible. "We need to be careful to wish for the right things, as we only have the three wishes."

His wife started to poke the fire and, without thinking about it, said, "What a lovely fire we have this evening. I wish we had a nice long string of juicy sausages to cook over it!" No sooner had she said this than her wish was granted. A string of sausages came tumbling down the chimney and landed on her lap. "Oh no! I didn't mean it as one of our wishes!" she moaned, looking at her husband. "What a waste of a wish!" he said. "How could you? I told you to be careful! I'm so furious with you, I wish the string of sausages was stuck to the end of your nose!"

# The three wishes

continued from previous page

No sooner had he said this than his wish was granted. The string of sausages flew up and stuck to the end of her nose. She pulled and pulled, but could not get the sausages off.

"I'm sorry," said the husband. "I didn't mean it as our second wish. We still have one wish left. I know, let's wish for so much money that we can make a gold box to put over your nose and the sausages." His wife was not at all pleased with this idea. "No!" she said "I'd rather hide away forever – you will never see me again." At this point her husband realized how much he loved his wife, more than any amount of gold or money. So he shrugged his shoulders, and told her to use up the third wish. She said, "I wish these sausages would drop off."

Well, of course they did drop off. They hugged each other, glad that they had each other. They had used up all three wishes; they still were not rich, but they had each other, and they spent an enjoyable evening cooking and eating the sausages.

## Preparation

Prepare a prop to represent the string of sausages, perhaps a stocking stuffed and tied in several places. An elastic loop at the top can be used to attach the sausages to the wife's face. Other useful props are a wand or wings for the fairy, an apron or bonnet for the wife, and a hat or jacket for the husband.

## Activity

Define an acting area and an audience area, where the non-actors will sit. As a whole group activity, set up the couple's living room. There is a fire, a chimney and two chairs where they sit. The group may add other items to create an atmosphere of simple homeliness. The sausages are placed off-stage.

There are three main roles to be filled: husband, wife and fairy, which can be played by a group in chorus. Other roles that can be played by group members are the fire, and the cottage itself. The rest of the group can be the audience. The group leader, as narrator, may ask the audience for help in retelling the story to encourage active involvement.

FAIRY TALES AND MYTHS

*10*

# The three wishes

## Guidelines for enactment scene by scene

1 The couple sit by their fire, warm their hands and chat. They begin to talk about their neighbours. The husband wishes there were fairies who could grant them all their wishes.

2 The fairy arrives, introduces herself, and grants them three wishes, with a warning to wish well. The fairy disappears.

3 The couple react to the visit by the fairy. They decide to be careful with their wishes.

4 The wife absent-mindedly wishes for a string of sausages, and they are sent down the chimney, perhaps by the fairy.

5 The husband reacts crossly and wishes the sausages stuck to his wife's nose.

6 The wife reacts with horror to the resulting predicament and threatens to hide away forever.

7 The husband lets her use up their last wish to get rid of the sausages. The sausages fall off. They embrace and spend the rest of the evening cooking and eating their sausages.

## Further development

What would each participant wish for if they met a fairy or djinn? Group members can take it in turns to play the role of the fairy, with the whole group creating a scene where the wish is fulfilled within the make-believe of the drama.

There are some profound themes in this story and the group facilitator should be mindful that they may need to be acknowledged and discussed in the group. In particular, the difficult feeling of shame in making a mistake, the disfigurement of the sausages on the nose, and the despair of wanting to hide away forever. A creative drama group can be a safe contained space for some of these personal resonances to be explored.

FAIRY TALES AND MYTHS 10

# Goldilocks and the three bears

## The narrative

Once upon a time there were three bears: a great big daddy bear, a medium-sized mummy bear and a small baby bear. They lived in a cottage in the woods. In this cottage they each had a bowl for their porridge: a great big one for daddy bear, a medium-sized one for mummy bear and a small one for baby bear. They each had their own chair to sit in: a great big one for daddy bear, a medium-sized one for mummy bear and a small one for baby bear. They also had their own bed to sleep in: a great big one for daddy bear, a medium-sized one for mummy bear and a small one for baby bear.

One morning they went for a walk in the woods while their porridge was cooling. That same morning a little girl was also walking in the woods. She was called Goldilocks, because she had golden curls and was very pretty. She was also very curious and, when she saw the cottage in the woods, she went up to it and peeped through the window. It looked like such a cosy cottage that she decided to take a closer look. She knocked on the door. No answer, so she opened the door and peeped inside. There was no-one there, but she could see the porridge on the table and went in to have a closer look.

Three bowls of porridge! It looked so delicious that she decided to taste a little. She tried the big bowl first, but it was too hot. Then she tried the medium-sized bowl, but it was too cold. Then she tried the small bowl and it was just right, so much so that she ate it all up.

Then she decided to sit down for a moment. First she tried the big chair, but it was too hard. Then she tried the medium-sized chair, but it was too soft. Then she tried the small chair, and it was just right. But it was only a small chair and it broke. She went upstairs and saw the three beds. First she tried the big bed, but she could not get comfortable in it. Then she tried the medium-sized bed, but she could not get comfortable in that one either. Then she lay down on the small bed and it was so comfortable that the moment her head touched the pillow she fell fast asleep.

A little later the three bears came home from their walk; they were looking forward to their porridge. They looked at the table and could see straight

# Goldilocks and the three bears

away that something was not right. The great big daddy bear said in his deep, gruff voice, "Somebody has been eating my porridge!" The mummy bear said in her medium voice, "Somebody has been eating my porridge!" And the baby bear said in its high voice, "Somebody has been eating my porridge, too, and they've eaten it all up!"

Then they looked at the chairs. "Somebody has been sitting on my chair!" said the big daddy bear in his deep, gruff voice. "Somebody has been sitting on my chair!" said the mummy bear in her medium voice. "Somebody has been sitting on my chair," said the baby bear in its high voice, "and they've broken it!" They went upstairs to see what they could find there, and looked at their three beds. "Somebody has been lying in my bed!" said the big daddy bear in his deep, gruff voice. "Somebody has been lying on my bed!" said the mummy bear in her medium voice. "Somebody has been lying on my bed, too," said the baby bear in its high voice, "and they're still in it!" At that moment Goldilocks woke up and saw the three bears by her bed. She was shocked. They were shocked. She screamed! They screamed! In all the pandemonium, she jumped out of the bed and ran as fast as she could out of the house, into the wood and back to wherever she came from. And that is the end of the story.

## Preparation

Assemble basic props: a table, three bowls, three chairs, and three blankets or cushions to represent the beds. Costumes for the bears can take the form of furry coats, jackets, hats or gloves. Half-masks can also be used, as long as they allow the actors to breathe freely, speak and see. The character of Goldilocks can be identified by a pinafore, skirt or cap.

## Activity

Define an acting area and an audience area. Set the scene as a whole group activity. Include an area for the wood as well as the cottage, with its table, three chairs and three beds. Other items can be added to make it seem homely and rural. As a whole group warm-up, practise the three bear voices in chorus, taking the lines from the porridge scene. Goldilocks' role can also be rehearsed collectively by going through her discovery and entry into the house in mime, emphasizing her wide-eyed curiosity. There are four main

# Goldilocks and the three bears

*continued from previous page*

roles to be filled: the three bears and Goldilocks. Other group members can be involved as the early morning wood, as trees, birds and sunshine.

## Guidelines for enactment scene by scene

1 The bears put their porridge on the table and set off for their walk.

2 The bears walk in the wood and hear the sounds of morning activity.

3 Goldilocks walks through the wood, discovers the house, peeps inside and enters.

4 She tries the three bowls of porridge, makes comments on each, and finishes off the small one.

5 She tries the three chairs, makes comments on each, and the third one breaks or falls over.

6 She tries the three beds, makes comments on each and falls asleep in the third one.

7 The bears return and notice the porridge bowls, one by one.

8 They notice the chairs, one by one.

9 They notice the beds, one by one. The baby bear finds Goldilocks, who wakes up. Everyone screams. She runs away.

● The story follows a predictable formula, and is well-known, so the group may be able to join in telling it. The enactment can be repeated several times, with different group members playing different roles. Audience members can join in the three bears' voices in chorus.

## Further development

The group finds an alternative ending for the story and enacts it. Perhaps the bears make friends with Goldilocks, and invite her to visit whenever they like; perhaps she is homeless and they invite her to live with them.

The themes of homelessness, feeling out of place and finding a place to belong may touch some group members at a profound level. Be prepared to discuss or at least acknowledge some of these issues that may emerge through the dramatic work.

CREATIVE DRAMA GROUPWORK FOR PEOPLE WITH LEARNING DIFFICULTIES

FAIRY TALES AND MYTHS

10

# The frog prince

## The narrative

Long ago and far away there lived a handsome young prince and his faithful servant Henry. One day a witch cast a spell on the prince, turning him into a frog. The only way the spell could be broken was if a princess let him eat from her plate and sleep on her pillow for three nights. It was hard to imagine a princess ever letting a frog sleep on her pillow, so the faithful servant Henry was very unhappy for his master, so much so that he thought his heart would break with sadness, and he tied three metal bands around his heart to hold it together.

Some time later a young princess, the youngest of three princesses, was playing in the woods near a spring with her favourite toy, a beautiful shining golden ball. She was very happy until the ball fell into the spring and disappeared in the water. The spring was deep and she could not see her ball, so she started to cry. She was very surprised when a frog appeared in the spring and asked her why she was crying. She was amazed to hear a frog talk and did not much like the look of him, but explained that she had lost her ball. "I will get your ball back for you," said the frog, "if you promise to love me, let me live with you, let me eat from your golden plate and let me sleep in your bed." "I promise," said the princess. The frog dived down and brought her the ball, but instead of taking the frog with her to fulfil her promise, she ran off home without another thought for him.

The next evening at the royal palace the royal family were eating their evening meal from their golden plates when there was a strange sound, a splish-splash, splish-splash, outside the dining hall, then a knock-knock-knock on the door. As the youngest, it was up to our princess to open the door. She was astonished and not at all happy to see the frog. She shut the door in its face and went back to the table. The frog knocked again and called through the door, "Don't forget your promise, princess, don't forget your promise!"

The king and her older sisters wanted to know what this was all about, and so the princess explained what had happened in the woods and that the frog was at the door. "You made a promise, and you must keep it," said the king, strictly. The princess was horrified, but obeyed. She opened the

FAIRY TALES AND MYTHS

# The frog prince

*continued from previous page*

door and the frog followed her to the table. She sat down. "Take me up!" demanded the frog. She tried to ignore him, but the king insisted. She let the frog onto her chair, and from there he jumped onto the table and ate from her plate. She thought this was disgusting, but there was worse to come. After the meal the frog said, "I'm tired now, take me to your bed!" The princess sat still, until her father the king reminded her, "You made a promise and you must keep it." Very reluctantly she went to her room with the frog. She put him on her pillow and kept her eyes on him all the time until she fell asleep.

The next day and the day after, the poor princess had to put up with the frog eating from her plate and sleeping on her pillow again. She was horrified and wished she had never made a promise. When she woke up after the third night, however, imagine her delight when she saw, instead of the frog on her pillow, a handsome prince standing by her bed. He explained his story to the princess, dropped to one knee and asked her solemnly to marry him. She said yes.

The next morning the faithful servant Henry arrived in a fine carriage drawn by white horses. The princess and her prince waved goodbye to the king and her sisters and drove off to the prince's kingdom, which was to be their new home. As they travelled along the road, they heard three loud cracks as, one by one, the bands around Henry's heart snapped. He was happy now, all was well, and there was no danger of his heart breaking.

## Preparation

Assemble some basic props and items of costume. Cut some long strips of aluminium foil for the metal bands around the servant's heart. The spring in the wood can be indicated with blue cloth or silver foil. An attractive shiny ball is needed for the princess. For the palace scene, paint some paper plates gold, and use fabric or cushions with rich texture and colour to indicate the opulence of the palace in both the dining hall and bedroom scenes. The horse-drawn carriage can be improvised with ropes for reins and cushions to sit on. The costumes can be kept simple: a black pointed hat and black cloak for the witch; a crown and cloak for the prince; green cloth for the frog, with a mask as a possible addition; a cape or shirt for Henry; crowns and cloths

# The frog prince

draped as long gowns for the princesses; the biggest crown for the King; and white cloths for manes and tails of the horses.

## Activity

The story can be told all at once or in stages over a period of sessions, depending on the attention span of the group and the time available. For each stage of the enactment, define audience and acting areas and set up the scenery for the make-believe world as a whole group activity. Let group members volunteer for specific roles, session by session. Involve the whole group in warm-up exercises to establish the characters, as suggested below, and when possible include subsidiary roles for those who want to be in the scene rather than watching.

## Guidelines for enactment scene by scene

1 The witch transforms the prince into a frog until such time as he wins the love of a princess. The distressed servant Henry binds his heart with three metal bands to stop it breaking.

For this opening scene all can explore and practise the essence of each of the characters: the witch's walk, laugh and voice as she casts her wicked spell; the prince's sudden transformation from regal stature to squatting frog; the servant's concern, sadness and fear that his heart will break.

2 The princess plays by the spring with her ball, loses it and cries. The frog gets her to make a promise and returns her ball. She goes home, leaving him in the wood. The whole group can practise the role of the princess, exploring different ways of playing with a ball. The sudden appearance of the frog and his dive through the water for the ball can be used as a framework for movement work for the whole group.

3 The evening meal in the royal palace is interrupted by the frog knocking at the door. After questions and explanations to her family, the princess reluctantly lets the frog join her at the table.

The whole group can be involved in creating an atmosphere of refinement and luxury in this scene. Apart from the three princesses and the king,

# The frog prince

*continued from previous page*

there can be any number of courtiers and servants, looking, moving and speaking as befits the royal setting. The dramatic contrast between this refined atmosphere and the apparent baseness of the frog is at the heart of this scene. Again the whole group can explore together an appropriately ungainly walk for the frog. Another opportunity for whole group involvement is provided by the group leader 'freezing' the scene and asking what the different characters are thinking or feeling. Do the older princesses relish seeing the younger one's embarrassment, or do they feel sorry for her? What are the king and the frog prince thinking?

**4** The princess reluctantly takes the frog to her bedroom, places him reluctantly on her pillow and lies down herself, being careful not to touch him, and keeping her eye on him until she falls asleep.

Set up the bedroom with a mat for the bed and a cushion for the pillow. The bed may be a luxurious four-poster, in which case four group members may take on the roles of the posts and drapery, and express their surprise, horror and distaste at the strange events in the princess's bedroom. Two players are required for the roles of princess and frog, each role backed up by a chorus of other group members, who express their thoughts and feelings: in the princess's case her sense of repugnance fighting with her sense of duty (for example, "I wish I could throw him out, but I promised"); in the frog's case, the strong wish that the spell could be broken and that he will return to his true form as a prince (for example, "If only she knew who I really am").

The scene is repeated twice; each time there is the possibility of recasting each of the roles. The transformation of frog into prince may be rehearsed by the whole group, before being played on the set. Work with the change of posture, from hunched and small to straight and tall. Removing a mask (or cloth used as a mask) or costume with a flourish at the same time adds to the dramatic impact. Perhaps the group as chorus can mark this moment with a loud "Tadaa!" The group may also work as a whole also to formulate the marriage proposal.

**5** The couple leave the palace in a coach driven by the trusty Henry. On the way to their new life, they hear the metal bands around his heart breaking

FAIRY TALES AND MYTHS

10

# The frog prince

and he explains that this is a sign that the sad times are over and the happy times have returned.

The whole group can be involved in both parts of this scene. As the couple leave the palace and say their goodbyes to the rest of the royal family and servants of the palace, there is an opportunity for everyone to express their feelings about goodbyes, whether they are one of those leaving or staying behind. Those who are not in role as Henry or the engaged couple can still be included in the journey into a happy future as one of the white horses pulling the carriage. This scene is the finale of the enactment and should, if possible, include everyone in the group. The spirit of relief and joy as happy times arrive can be expressed in movement, in song or with musical instruments.

## Further development

There are powerful themes in this story. For some groups it may be enough to explore these themes indirectly through the enactment, without specific thematic discussion afterwards. Others may wish to have time to discuss some of these themes and their personal relevance. Examples are a favourite toy, promises, saying no, marriage, being good enough, sadness and relief. These themes could be developed further in dramatic improvisation or further stories.

For example, re-playing the bedroom scene in terms of the princess saying no to the frog *despite* the promise and the father's insistence she keep it could be an important step in terms of assertiveness for some individuals and groups. We have to learn to trust ourselves sometimes more than a higher authority!

- Group leaders may wish to re-write the story from the outset to emphasize certain learning points. Fairy tales have always been subject to change. Group leaders and group members should free to explore the story's potential in a number of ways.

# Hansel and Gretel

## The narrative

Once upon a time, at the edge of a large wood, there lived two children with their father, a woodcutter, and their stepmother. The boy's name was Hansel and the girl was called Gretel. They were very, very poor and often had to go without food. One evening, when the children had gone to bed, the stepmother spoke to her husband. "There simply isn't enough food for four people. We must get rid of those children or we will all starve. We'll take them into the wood tomorrow and leave them there." The woodcutter was horrified at this idea because he loved his children, and the wood was full of dangerous wild animals who would surely kill and eat poor Hansel and Gretel, but his wife insisted and eventually he agreed to the plan.

The two children were lying in bed, too hungry to sleep, and they heard their parents talking. Gretel was frightened and cried, but Hansel said, "Don't worry, Gretel. I have an idea." When the house was quiet and everyone was sleeping, he got up, put on his coat and crept quietly outside into the night. The moon was shining and the white pebbles on the ground shone brightly in the moonlight. Hansel picked up as many as he could cram into his pockets, then went back inside to bed.

The next morning the stepmother gave the two children a piece of dry bread each to last them the day and they all set off to chop wood. They walked for a long time, further and further into the wood, turning first one way, then the other. The stepmother was sure the children would never be able to find their way back to the house, but all the time Hansel was dropping the white pebbles in his pockets onto the path.

At last they stopped walking and built a fire together. The stepmother told the children to wait by the fire while she and their father chopped wood. "We will come and get you when we have finished our work," she lied. Hansel and Gretel sat by the fire, ate their bread and waited. They waited and waited, and eventually fell asleep. When they woke up it was night time and very dark. "We'll never find our way home now," cried Gretel. "Wait for the moon to come up," said Hansel. "Don't worry." At last the moon rose. Hansel took his sister's hand and together they followed the trail of white pebbles he had dropped along the path, which shone like silver in

CREATIVE DRAMA GROUPWORK FOR PEOPLE WITH LEARNING DIFFICULTIES

# Hansel and Gretel

the moonlight. They walked all night and arrived home at daybreak. Their stepmother was surprised and not very pleased to see them, but their father was relieved and happy.

They lived together again for a few weeks, but were very poor and hungry. One evening, after the children had gone to bed, the stepmother spoke to their father and said, "I've had enough. We must get rid of them properly this time. We shall go even further into the wood so they can't get back. No arguments – I have decided we shall do it tomorrow." She stood up, locked the front door and went to bed. Hansel and Gretel had heard all this from their bed. Again Hansel got up to go and collect pebbles from outside, but this time the door was locked and he could not get out. "Don't worry, Gretel," he said, as he came back to bed, "we'll find a way."

Early next morning the stepmother gave them each a small piece of bread and they all set off early for the woods. They walked this way and that, further and further into the woods. This time, without any white pebbles to drop, Hansel dropped crumbs of bread on the path in the hope that they would be able to follow the track of crumbs in the moonlight later. He did not notice that every time he dropped a crumb the hungry birds in the wood would swoop down and eat it. When they got to the heart of the wood they all built a fire and the children sat by it as their parents went off to chop wood. They shared Gretel's bread, waited and waited, fell asleep and woke up when it was dark and the moon rising.

"Don't worry, Gretel," Hansel said, "follow me!" He started to look for the bread crumbs on the path, but there was nothing to be seen. They walked and walked all night, and all next day, but did not find the path. They were lost in the wood. Eventually, exhausted and weak from hunger, they lay down under a tree and slept. Next day they saw a beautiful white bird, singing in a tree. As it spread its wings and flew off, Hansel said, "Let's follow that bird. Maybe it can show us the way. If we don't find help soon we will die." They followed the bird until it landed on a pretty little cottage standing on its own in the middle of the wood. The children were amazed to see the cottage was made of bread and cakes and sweets. It was like a dream come true. They were so hungry they broke whole pieces off the roof and windows and started to munch.

# Hansel and Gretel

• • • • • • • • • • • • • • • • • • • • • • • • • • • • • • • • • • • • • • • • • • • • • •

*continued from previous page*

They were startled by the voice of an old woman standing in the doorway. "Welcome, dear children, come inside and let me make you something to eat. I will take care of you. Come!" They followed her inside, not realizing that she was a witch. She made them pancakes and let them sleep in two comfortable beds, but all the time she was laughing to herself, thinking, "What tasty looking children these are. What a lovely meal I shall make of them." Witches have very bad eyesight, so she waited until Hansel and Gretel lay sleeping, then crept up and had a close look at them. "They need fattening up," she thought. "At least I shall make a good meal out of one of them." She grabbed Hansel roughly, dragged him out of bed and locked him in a cage. Hansel screamed, but it was no use. Then she woke up Gretel and told her to fetch water. They were going to cook a nice meal for Hansel so that he would get fat and tasty. She ordered Gretel to do this and do that and, although Gretel did not want to, she had no choice. Hansel was given plates of food, and Gretel was given scraps. This went on for weeks, and every morning the witch would go to Hansel's cage and tell him to poke out his finger so that she could feel if he was getting fat. Hansel would stick out a thin bone left over from one of his meals. The witch could not understand why he was still so thin despite all the food.

At last she had had enough of waiting. Fat or thin, it was time he was eaten. "Get some water, Gretel," she ordered. "We're cooking him now." Gretel cried but it was no use. When she came back with the water, the witch lit the oven and opened the door to it. "Gretel, climb in the oven and tell me if it's hot enough," she said, thinking, "Once she's in the oven, I'll shut the door on her and have her as a tasty side dish." Gretel was suspicious, and asked the witch to show her how to get into the oven. "Silly girl," said the witch, "it's easy. There's even room for me to put my head in." The witch bent over to show Gretel, who pushed the witch with all her strength into the oven and shut the door on her.

As the witch howled in the oven, Gretel ran to her brother's cage and opened it. They hugged each other, then looked around the witch's house, which was full of treasure. They took as much as Hansel could cram into his pockets and Gretel hold in her apron, then left the witch's house. They walked for a while until they came to a large stretch of water. There was no bridge and it was too far to swim, so they could not think how to get across.

# Hansel and Gretel

Then a white duck came swimming by and they called to it to help them across the water.

"Help us, duck! Please don't hide! Help us get to the other side." The duck came to them and Hansel climbed on. "Come, too!" he called to Gretel. "That would be too much for the duck," replied his sister. "You go ahead alone, and then the duck can come back for me." They had always been together until now, but Hansel agreed and so the duck carried them across the water one at a time. They thanked the duck and went on their way.

Before long they recognized a path back to the woodcutter's house, and started to run. When they arrived home their father hugged them, delighted to see them again. He told them that their stepmother had died after they left them in the wood. The children told their father their story and showed him all the treasure they had brought back from the witch's house. They would never be poor or hungry again, and they lived happily ever after.

## Preparation

Assemble basic props: empty bowls for the first scene; a torch or white paper disc for the moon; some real pebbles for the first journey; twigs or canes for the fires in the wood; real bread or pieces of foam sponge for both journeys into the wood; coloured cloths and shapes for the outside of the witch's house; a pot or jug for Gretel to fetch water in; a stick or real bone for Hansel's bone; marbles and beads for treasure; and blue cloth for the lake. The costumes can be kept simple: a peasant's hat, gloves and a belt with a cardboard axe for the woodcutter; a dark shawl for the stepmother; a jacket for Hansel; an apron for Gretel; white cloth for the moon; yellow cloth for the sun; a shawl and witch's hat for the witch and white cloth to drape for the bird and duck.

## Activity

This story is too long for most groups to listen to in one go, and is best approached as a project over several sessions, allowing enough time for de-roling at the end of each. Read the relevant passages as an introduction to each scene. Define an acting and audience area, and set up the scene as

# Hansel and Gretel

*continued from previous page*

a whole group activity. As well as the main roles, there are opportunities for smaller roles: the moon, sun, fire, birds and trees in the wood, bars of the witch's cage and the witch's oven. There is also scope for the whole group to prepare and rehearse key moments in each scene. Encourage volunteers for the key roles session by session.

## Guidelines for enactment scene by scene

1 The family sit hungry with empty bowls. Hansel and Gretel go to bed and lie awake listening to their parents' plan to abandon them. When the moon comes up, Hansel goes and collects stones.

The scene can be set with four areas: the living room, the children's bedroom, the parents' bedroom and the area outside the front door. Add to the atmosphere if possible by adjusting the lighting. The moon can be portrayed by a group member draped in white, holding a disc or torch.

Before enacting the scene, the group can build up the atmosphere by splitting into pairs. Each pair lies down and pretends to sleep while having a conversation in whispers. Hansel's journey outside and back to bed can form the basis of a game for the whole group. Half the group close their eyes while the other half try to creep silently past them without being heard.

2 The family journey into the wood, Hansel dropping stones on the way. They make a fire and the parents go off to chop wood. The children eat, sleep and wake. The moon rises and they follow the stones back home. Father greets them, the stepmother sneers.

As well as the main roles, one or more participants can play the part of the fire and someone the moon. Others can play woodland creatures such as squirrels and rabbits in the daytime, and owls and foxes by night. The first journey through the wood can be made into a version of 'Follow my Leader'. The creatures of the wood may watch Hansel and Gretel from their hiding places or join in the line of people walking through the wood. Similarly, for the journey back the creatures of the wood may or may not help Hansel and Gretel.

# Hansel and Gretel

3 The stepmother insists that she and her husband try and lose the children again, so the family goes into the wood a second time, Hansel dropping bread crumbs. The birds eat them. The parents leave the children by the fire again and they eat, sleep and wake in the dark. The moon rises but there is nothing to be seen. They wander, lost, for a night and a day, until they fall asleep under a tree.

There are elements of this scene which are familiar. The group can emphasize both the similarities with the previous scene and the differences. The whole group can be involved in the episode with the birds. They can also help to create the passage of time. As the moon sets, the sun can rise, and after the sun sets for a second time the children sleep. Sunrise and sunset can be represented by lifting or lowering a large yellow cloth held by two group members. Other group members can take on the roles of daytime and night-time animals again. When Hansel and Gretel finally fall asleep, the whole forest can sleep too, creating a peaceful ending to the group enactment of this scene.

4 Hansel and Gretel follow the bird and find the witch's house. They eat bits of the house. The witch invites them in and cooks for them, then shows them to their beds.

This scene requires three settings: the woods, the outside of the house and the inside of the house. Building the outside of the house in particular is a creative challenge for the whole group.

The dramatic essence of the scene is the contrast between the children's sense of good fortune in finding the bird, the house and old woman's hospitality and the actual evil intentions of the witch. All is not what it seems. One way of working on this dramatically is to split the witch into two roles, the mask of false hospitality that she presents to the children, and the reality of her wicked intentions. If one group member plays both roles she can hold up a pleasant mask when talking to the children, and drop it when voicing the witch's thoughts to herself. If two group members play the double role, one plays the hospitable old woman, the other the laughing, scheming witch, hiding behind the 'nice' one, but visible to the audience.

# Hansel and Gretel

*continued from previous page*

**5** The witch examines the sleeping children, decides they are too thin, imprisons Hansel and enslaves Gretel. She orders Gretel to prepare a meal to fatten Hansel. The witch checks whether he is getting fatter, but he confuses her by holding out a thin bone through the cage to represent his finger.

As role preparation, the whole group can work together on the orders the witch gives Gretel to prepare the meal for Hansel, paying attention to the voice and gestures suited to the witch. The bars of the cage can be represented by group members standing close together or with linked arms.

**6** The witch decides to cook Hansel. She lights the oven and asks Gretel to climb in to test the temperature. Gretel tricks the witch and pushes her into the oven. While the witch screams, Gretel frees Hansel and together they gather up the witch's treasures and leave the house.

When setting the scene, include the treasure. As with the cage in the previous scene, the oven can be represented by several group members crouching close together. This creates a softer environment for the witch to be trapped in, and the oven itself can magnify the witch's screams in chorus. There is also a role for fire again inside the oven, represented by a group member with a red cloth, which starts small as the witch lights the oven, then grows and eventually envelops the witch.

**7** The children come across a large stretch of water. They call to a passing duck to help them cross it, which they do one at a time. They find their old home and are reunited with their father, to whom they show their treasure.

Two settings are required for this scene; the water in the woods and the woodcutter's house. The children call to the duck in rhyme (See p. 000). The whole group can learn and join in this chant together. In the story, the duck carries each child across the water on its back. If possible, the person playing the duck can be on all fours, with Hansel and Gretel sitting on his back. If that is physically inappropriate, Hansel and Gretel can each sit on a cushion, blanket or trolley on wheels and be pulled through the water. It can be a group task to find the best way of staging the scene by

FAIRY TALES AND MYTHS

*10*

See p. 000

CREATIVE DRAMA GROUPWORK FOR PEOPLE WITH LEARNING DIFFICULTIES

# Hansel and Gretel

exploring different ways of taking each other across the work space as if through water.

## Further development

The story is rich in themes which can be the basis for discussion or further dramatic exploration through improvisation: for example, friendship and mutual support, coming through difficult times, knowing who to trust, family relationships and becoming independent.

# The story of the seasons – Demeter and Persephone

This story comes from Ancient Greece, and as well as being about the origin of the seasons it introduces us to the Greek gods – about whom there are a multitude of exciting stories, which you might be inspired to explore. Themes within this story are mother–daughter relationships, man–woman relationships, loss and grief, force and choice, betrayal and reconciliation, life and death.

## Meeting the gods – the main characters

Zeus – king of all the gods. Used to getting his own way, strong, and not always very thoughtful of others.

Demeter – his sister, in charge of the harvest, makes sure things grow and that we can all eat. Her nature is loving, caring and generous.

Demeter's daughter Persephone – young, innocent, but growing into womanhood, playful and enjoys life with her mother and friends.

Demeter's friends she enjoys playing with.

Hades – god of the underworld, powerful, wealthy, and lonely, longing for a wife.

Hermes – messenger of the gods, very good at communicating, a good talker, quick on his feet (actually his feet have wings so he can move fast).

Helios – the sun god who gives light and warmth, helps things to grow, and can see whatever is going on above ground.

## The narrative

Long ago in Ancient Greece, Demeter was making sure that the world was fertile – crops were growing, seeds were germinating, fruit ripening on the trees. Flowers blossomed, bees buzzed as they collected honey. Animals had enough to eat and drink, there was the sound of busy life. People were working the fields, tending their animals, feasting together and enjoying each other's company. There was plenty, and life was good.

Demeter's daughter Persephone was playing in the fields with her friends, exploring the flowers and fruits, and Demeter was very proud of her and loved her deeply.

CREATIVE DRAMA GROUPWORK FOR PEOPLE WITH LEARNING DIFFICULTIES

# The story of the seasons –
# Demeter and Persephone

Life was good and bright and Helios the sun looked at everything, helped it grow and gave warmth to the world.

Meanwhile, in a very different place, Hades ruled in the shady underworld, the place where the dead rested. He was king there, very powerful. He had comfort, riches, servants, good food from the world above . . . but no one special to share it with. He was lonely.

One day he visited the world above and watched Persephone with her friends. He decided that he wanted her to be his bride. He knew that her mother would never agree to her going to live with him in the dark underworld, so he spoke to Zeus, the king of the gods, about his plans, and Zeus agreed to his plan to abduct her.

It happened like this: Persephone and her friends were picking flowers to take to Demeter, as a gift. A wonderful scent from a special flower caught Persephone's attention, and she followed it, leaving her friends behind. As she bent down to pick the flower, the earth beneath her feet opened, there was a rumble, like thunder, and suddenly Hades appeared, speeding along on his chariot. She hardly had time to open her mouth in astonishment and fear before he had swooped her up and they were gone, into the dark underworld.

Persephone called out to her mother to help her, but she was already too far away for anyone to hear.

When Demeter noticed that her daughter was missing she was distraught. She roamed the countryside, calling to Persephone, going to all her favourite places. She did not rest for days and nights. She asked everyone she came across if they knew what had happened, but no-one knew, no-one saw.

She was worried, angry, and then she felt helpless and low. She stopped tending the crops, and making sure that there was food for everyone. She didn't care anymore. The crops stopped growing. Soon there would be

# The story of the seasons – Demeter and Persephone

*continued from previous page*

famine, the animals and the people would starve. There was a fog of sadness all over the world. Everything had changed.

At last she asked the sun, Helios, what he knew. Surely, he could see everything that happens on earth. Helios took pity on Demeter and told her about the conversation between Hades and Zeus, and how Hades had taken Persephone to the underworld in his chariot to be his bride.

Imagine Demeter's feelings to hear that all this had been arranged behind her back, and that her beloved daughter was gone. She marched off to Mount Olympus where Zeus lived and called up to him – "That's it, I'm done. There will be no more crops until I am reunited with my daughter." Zeus started to worry. If the people couldn't eat, they would be angry with him and stop worshipping him – and he loved to be worshipped. He was king of the gods. He called his messenger Hermes, and told him to go to Hades and try and sort something out.

Meanwhile, down in Hades Persephone was longing for home and her mother. She was in a most beautiful room, full of fine furniture, beautiful clothes. She was waited on hand and foot and Hades was very charming to her, taking her for trips around his kingdom and letting her know how much she would be valued if she agreed to be his queen. She knew that she mustn't eat anything in the underworld – everyone knew that once you have eaten in the underworld there is no going back! She was determined not to eat. At the same time, she was beginning to grow fond of Hades, and the people of his underworld.

One day, Hermes was just arriving in Hades and he could see Hades and Persephone sitting together on a sofa. Hades was offering Persephone fruit, a ripe and juicy pomegranate. He could see her from a distance shaking her head, and pushing the platter of fruit away. Then he saw Hades offering again, trying to persuade her to keep her strength up. Slowly, and deliberately she took six pomegranate seeds from the platter, and popped them in her mouth. Oh no, she was now committed to stay here. What would Zeus say if Hermes failed to sort out a solution.

FAIRY TALES AND MYTHS

10

# The story of the seasons – Demeter and Persephone

Hermes stepped forward to talk to Hades. "I know that Persephone has eaten six seeds, and that she now belongs to the underworld, but I come from Zeus himself, king of the gods. He has asked me to bring Persephone back to be with her mother, so that the crops will flourish and the people will not starve. We need to find a way for this to happen." Hades turned to Persephone and asked her, "Will you go back for six months, to be with your mother and the world of light, then return to me for six months, one for each of the six seeds you have eaten to be my queen?" Persephone agreed, Hermes was happy and Zeus in the distance breathed a big sigh of relief.

And that was how it happened. Persephone became queen of the underworld, returning to Demeter for the summer, when everything was happy and fruitful. In the autumn every year she went back to Hades, the world became a darker place, leaves fell, rains came, the crops stopped growing. Demeter missed her, but knew that she would come back again in Spring, when the cycle of the seasons began all over again. And that is how the seasons came to be.

## Preparation

Assemble some basic props – pictures of the Greek countryside will help as an introduction to the world depicted in the story. You may also add pictures of the Greek gods. For the enactment – flowers, fruit (including a pomegranate if available), real or artificial; a thunder drum or similar to announce the arrival of Hades; coloured cloths for the two worlds – bright colours for Demeter's world and greys, black, silver for the underworld, a yellow cloth for Helios, gold crown for Zeus and a silver one for Hades.

## Activity

The story lends itself to activity over a few sessions. You might spend a session just working on meeting the main characters, and establishing the world or worlds of the story. There are three different locations that can be explored dramatically, before the story is enacted. Zeus on his high mountain; Demeter, Persephone, and the world of vegetation, animals and humans;

# The story of the seasons – Demeter and Persephone

*continued from previous page*

and the shady underworld with Hades, his servants and all the people who have ever lived and died. The story itself makes a link between all of these worlds, linking life and death and the seasons.

## Guidelines for enactment scene by scene

1 Meeting the gods. Get to know the characters through movement exploration. Everyone who wants to can practise being Zeus – the one in charge of all the gods, the boss! How does he walk and talk, and what's it like looking down from his high mountain at the world below? Similarly, everyone can explore the role of Helios – giving warmth and light, and noticing everything that happens. The role of Demeter involves blessing and encouraging all of life – this role can be explored in turn by different group members, whilst the others find movement expression for growth (crops, trees, seeds turning to flowers), and bees gathering nectar for honey, animals eating the grain or grass, and people working the fields. The role of Hades involves power, a somewhat imposing and scary presence, but in his own way dignified and attractive – an interesting role for exploration as a group, using facial expression and long strides to capture his status as king of the underworld. Hermes is quick, clever, and light – moving fast wherever Zeus tells him to go. Persephone, the heroine of the story, is curious, inquisitive, playful and friendly – she enjoys exploring her world.

2 Demeter and Helios oversee the fruitfulness of the world. People are planting and harvesting, animals are eating, the sun is shining, bees are buzzing. Persephone and her friends go off exploring, picking flowers, smelling their scent. They are collecting a bunch of flowers to give to Demeter.

This scene can be built up bit by bit and might be supported by harmonious music.

3 Hades visits from the underworld, looks at Persephone and wants to have her as his bride. He asks Zeus what he thinks, and Zeus says go ahead, do what you like. We might wonder what he was thinking; certainly he wasn't thinking about either Demeter or Persephone. For whatever reason he gives his blessing to Hades to abduct Persephone.

CREATIVE DRAMA GROUPWORK FOR PEOPLE WITH LEARNING DIFFICULTIES

FAIRY TALES AND MYTHS

*10*

# The story of the seasons – Demeter and Persephone

4 The abduction – as Persephone follows the scent to find a special flower, she moves away from her friends. There is the sound of thunder and the earth opens. With an impressive fanfare Hades arrives in his chariot and disappears again into the underworld with Persephone.

This scene offers the opportunity for some musical improvisation to make the sound of Hades' arrival. Also for some movement work, the earth opening can be depicted through several group members lying on the floor and rolling outwards to create a channel for Hades to drive through – and rolling back once he has taken Persephone. The same effect might be achieved by using cloths to show the world splitting apart and darkness emerging from the light.

5 Demeter's search for Persephone – asking everyone she sees where Persephone is, whether they have seen anything. Eventually she becomes so sad that she stops helping the world to grow food. All the crops dry up and wither, the animals go hungry, and the people start to worry where their food will come from. A sad and desperate time.

This scene is all about searching and asking. The whole group can work together on running to each other, looking for Persephone and asking "Where is she?" Similarly the gradual drying up of the crops can be explored as a whole group, through movement sequences of drying up, shrivelling.

6 The conversation with Helios, the sun god, and the truth is revealed. Demeter's angry confrontation with Zeus, and Zeus sends his messenger off to Hades, to try and fix things.

7 Hades courts Persephone, tries to tempt her with food, and she always says no, but begins to warm to him and to the idea of being queen of the underworld. Finally, just as Hermes arrives and watches, she accepts the pomegranate seeds and eats them. She is now committed to Hades and the underworld. Hades and Hermes work out a solution, that Persephone will return to earth for six months, then back to him for six months. The cycle of the seasons is established.

# The story of the seasons – Demeter and Persephone

*continued from previous page*

This scene is the climax of the drama. The offer of food and refusal to eat can be repeated several times, to build up to the decisive moment when Persephone pops the seeds in her mouth. Hermes watches, much as Hades watched the scene of the friends playing in the earlier scene. The group leader/narrator can guide the group's attention from the action on the sofa, to the action of Hermes observing.

8 The dance of the seasons – the cycle of the seasons is celebrated with a circle dance, in which the sun and the bounty of Spring and Summer are followed by the sadness and darkness of autumn and winter, as Persephone returns to the underworld until Spring comes again. Both Hades and Demeter have their moments of prominence, as Persephone dances with them.

## Further development

Find out what the favourite seasons are for group members, and why. Each season has its own beauty and mood.

At a personal level, group members may be invited to reflect on their own experiences of loss. They may name people, places or things they have lost and explore words and gestures for the feelings they had at the time.

You might also explore the passage of time, how certain times of the year are special to us and then they are over, until they come around again, and also the process of growing older. As a little girl Persephone stayed close to her mother, then learned to become more independent as she grew up. Group members might reflect on steps they too have taken towards independence.

CREATIVE DRAMA GROUPWORK FOR PEOPLE WITH LEARNING DIFFICULTIES

# Performance

# Performance

## Choice of audience

Once the decision to perform is made, the next step is to consider the nature of the audience who will see the show. The possibilities can be discussed in the group. There are three types of audience to be considered. The first is small and local. This audience is familiar with the performers and with the space, including, for example, other service users, another class and colleagues in the same agency. The second type is a small invited public. This audience includes known, familiar people from outside the agency, such as family members, friends and colleagues. Finally, there is the wider public. This audience includes anyone interested and attracted to the show by publicity or word of mouth.

Discuss which option the group is most attracted to and whether the risk level is tolerable. Consider also whether the size of audience would influence the choice of performance space. If a group is used to working in one space, it can be difficult to move the work to another space for performance. Each space has different acoustic qualities and a different atmosphere. Familiarity with a space gives confidence, so for minimum stress a performance in the regular creative drama space is recommended, especially for first-time performers. If this is not appropriate, do allow plenty of time for settling into a new space and making appropriate adaptations in performance style and staging.

## Scheduling the work

The performance date may already be known at the start of a project – for example, if it is to coincide with a fixed event. In this case it is a matter of devising a performance which can be done in the time allowed. If the performance date is to be decided by the group, ensure that this is done as early on in the project as possible, to give the work process a framework. As soon as the performance date is established, the group can make a chart outlining the number of weeks or number of sessions until the performance. At the start of each session, the group can focus on their position on the schedule, and a group member can mark the current session. This ritual keeps the idea of a future performance date alive in the group, builds up excitement and focus as the date approaches and reminds the group what has been achieved so far.

PERFORMANCE

*11*

# Performance

● ● ● ● ● ● ● ● ● ● ● ● ● ● ● ● ● ● ● ● ● ● ● ● ● ● ● ● ● ● ● ● ● ● ● ● ● ● ● ● ● ● ● ● ● ● ●

*continued from previous page*

The schedule is a reminder of the shared responsibility in the group. It is only of value if group members agree to be present at sessions as required and to give their support to the work. The sense of the schedule as a shared contract can be highlighted at the outset by asking all group members, including the group leader, to sign the chart as a symbol of their personal commitment to the group project.

## Pacing the work

The performance is prepared within a fixed period of time. It is important that the task can be accomplished in the time allowed so that group members can put themselves forward with confidence. The group leader, as director, needs an overview of the work required for the show to be ready. Flexibility and the ability to deviate from preconceived plans are also necessary. It is realistic to expect some group members to have off days and possible absences. If the rehearsal schedule is too tightly paced, these hiccups create more tension than if the director is generous and realistic with time from the outset. The rehearsal process is a learning process, one which takes time and practice. Even if scenes are to be partially improvised in performance, the actors need a well-grounded familiarity with the core elements. Each rehearsal may include new elements as well as a repetition of familiar elements, to keep them fresh in mind and perhaps to further refine them. At the end of a session, it can be helpful to remind the group what they have achieved so far and what was new in the session.

Time should also be built into the schedule for designing and distributing publicity material and programmes, and for making scenery, props and costumes as necessary. This practical 'hands on' work creates variety in the rehearsal and preparation process and helps make the idea of a future performance more concrete.

## Models of performance projects

### Sharing work in progress

This model of performance is relatively low-key. The performance is regarded as an opportunity to show an audience the kind of work done in the creative drama sessions. A number of familiar drama structures can be performed for their own sake, without a particular story holding them

# Performance

together. Some continuity can be created through the role of master of ceremonies, who introduces each structure by title and may say a few words about it. This role can be shared amongst several group members or taken on by the group leader as a continuous thread throughout the performance. If the group is particularly anxious, the intermittent appearance of the group leader as master of ceremonies holding the show together can be reassuring.

The particular structures chosen for performance can reflect the group's own favourite drama activities. To minimize anxiety, start with activities performed by the group as a whole, so that everyone has the chance to warm up to performing. Gradually move towards more differentiated and demanding structures, and end with a finale involving the whole group. There follows a sample programme based on structures described in previous chapters.

## Part 1: Warm-up

1 Group Hum (see p. 105). The group make a sound improvisation together.

2 Introduction Game (see p. 36). Each person introduces themselves to the group and audience.

3 Throwing the Voice (see p. 102). Using a large ball, group members call to each other.

4 Body Parts (see p. 30). This can be led by the group leader. Alternatively, each member of the group leads the exercise for one body part, with the rest of the group following. Each time leadership changes, the previous leader calls the next leader by name, so that leadership is clearly passed on.

## Part 2: Action

1 A journey (see 'Travellers', p. 173). This scene is based on what was originally an improvisation, which is then to some extent 'fixed' through rehearsal. The group knows beforehand where they are going, what props and scenery are required, who plays which individual roles and what is expected of them in each phase. The journey follows the three-part structure of travelling, being there and returning.

# Performance

continued from previous page

## Part 3: Closure

1 Circle Dance (see p. 64).

2 Choreographed curtain call. The performance benefits from a clear, rehearsed finish in which individuals and the group as a whole bow, receive applause and make their exit.

### Devised show around a theme

In this kind of performance the bulk of the material consists of a number of scenes relating either to the same characters appearing in each scene, to a particular place or to a chosen theme. Flexible themes include family, the life cycle, work and modes of transport. A warm-up and closure scene may or may not relate to the main theme. There follow two sample outlines. The first is for the family.

## Part 1: Warm-up

1 Family photos (see 'Statues', p. 73). The whole group moves into and out of three contrasting group sculptures, as if posing for a formal family photograph. Hats, pieces of costume and props can be included to give distinctive character and variety. One person takes the role of photographer, using a flash (or real camera) to capture the moment when each photographic pose comes to stillness. The moment after the flash, the group disbands and reforms as a different family image.

## Part 2: Action

Having tried out a number of improvisations around the theme of family relationships (see 'A Family Get-together', p. 181), the group chooses a few to rehearse, refine and perform, for example as follows:

1 Breakfast time at the Smith family.

2 Sam Smith's first day at school.

3 Sam and Samira Smith play with their friends next door.

4 The Smith family receive a message via email, phone or letter (they have won a lottery, or inherited money from a rich relative).

# Performance

**5** A family argument (between the parents or the children or the grandparents, or between different generations).

**6** A family celebration (a birthday party, a wedding, a celebration of their newfound wealth).

## Part 3: Closure

As a group, participants devise a song about families in general or about the Smith family in particular. They accompany the song with instruments and choreographed dance movements, then make a clear, theatrical ending, followed by a bow.

The second sample outline is for going places. This piece is based on different ways of getting from A to B.

## Part 1: Warm-up

**Walking:** one after another, participants enter the stage area and walk about until the whole group is on stage. Some walk alone, others arm-in-arm, in pairs. Each person walks sometimes slowly, sometimes fast, sometimes in straight lines, sometimes in curves. Changes in tempo and mood can be indicated by the group leader striking a gong or beating a drum. After an agreed and rehearsed number of phases, the final cue is for the whole group to freeze.

## Part 2: Action

Each scene involves a simple change of scenery indicating the new location and mode of transport.

**Scene 1: Boat** This can be a punt, rowing boat, sailing boat or ocean liner. Some participants create the atmosphere, movements and sound effects of the location. Others play the characters on board and, if applicable, on land. Choose a dramatically clear moment to close the scene: for example, after much preparation the boat finally leaves harbour; after days of drifting at sea, land is finally spotted; or a dreamy lover on a punt falls into the river.

**Scene 2: Train** A train can be a good setting for a mystery or detective story. Something or someone may go missing during the temporary blackout

# Performance

*continued from previous page*

of a tunnel. There is good scope for interesting characters: detective, suspect passengers, rail personnel, victim, criminal. The scene may end conventionally, with the clever detection of the guilty party, or unexpectedly, with a further crime.

**Scene 3: Aeroplane** Journeys by aeroplane are full of ritual (see 'Travelling by Plane', p. 124). These start at the airport with checking in, weighing the baggage and going through passport control, and continue on the aeroplane with fastening seat belts, a welcome from the cabin staff and crew, safety demonstrations, take-off, meals and landing. A story-line can be developed using the idea of a family or group of friends flying off to the sun for a holiday. After the lengthy process of the journey, they finally arrive at their chosen destination, which may or may not be everything they have dreamed of.

**Scene 4: Rocket or spaceship** A space journey is a wonderful opportunity for the group to explore fantasy. Actors can wear real costume spacesuits or indicate them in mime. After countdown and blast-off, everyone moves in slow motion. Electronic music can be used to help create the atmosphere of otherworldliness. The destination may be the moon or a fantasy planet. Once this destination is reached, some space travellers leave the rocket and explore the new environment. Perhaps they meet alien beings. Anything is possible. The end of the scene can be the return to the rocket and the countdown for the journey home.

## Part 3: Closure

Choreographed curtain call. After all the work in character, in this closure everyone returns to their own identity. Starting from as far back as possible in a line, each person performs their own movement pattern as a way of coming to the front of the stage and taking a bow. When all have arrived, a second bow is taken by all together.

### Performance of a single story

In this type of performance, one story forms the basis of the whole show. This can be a known story worked on and refined in stages over a period of time following the model of Noah's Ark (see p. 185). The same process can be applied to fairy tales (see *Chapters 7* and *10*, on puppets and fairy tales).

CREATIVE DRAMA GROUPWORK FOR PEOPLE WITH LEARNING DIFFICULTIES

# Performance

The performance can also be based on a story invented by the group through an improvisation, which is subsequently rehearsed and refined over a period of time (see *Chapter 8*, on improvisation).

In a single story performance there can be a sense of satisfaction in creating a unified whole. The sequence of scenes is determined by the plot and each part of the show is indispensable. In the other models of performance, the absence of one performer may jeopardize one scene, while allowing the show as a whole to go ahead. Where the performance is based on a single story, the absence of a key performer could put the whole performance at risk, a fact which can create an added sense of pressure in the group.

# 12

# De-roling

# Physical de-roling

## Marking the moment

As an enactment draws to a close, the group leader looks for an appropriate moment to give the direction to "freeze". With practice the participants will come to a point of stillness and the dramatic action will cease. The group leader invites them to close their eyes and announces that the enactment is now over and that it is time to return to the here and now. During a period of five seconds the group can prepare to let go of the imaginary roles and the imaginary context of the enactment. The group leader counts out loud and on reaching zero welcomes the group back to their familiar roles.

## Laying aside the trappings of a role

The dramatic role is often symbolized by a piece of costume or a prop which helps the performer to find and enter a role. The role exists usually in the context of a dramatic setting, which may be as simple as a chair in an empty space. When the time comes to step out of the imaginary world, it helps to remove these items of costume and to dismantle the set.

If the items used have familiar places in the creative drama space, part of the ritual can be to return them to these places, where they are de-roled. A hat that represented the bandit or the bridesmaid role in an enactment is returned to its usual place where its function is neutral until it is used again.

Periods of transition can be confusing and disturbing for people with learning difficulties. By creating a time and a sequence in the session for the process of laying aside the trappings of the imaginary role, the group leader can support participants through any difficulties and help keep the group as a whole focused.

## Further development

Before removing pieces of costume, the group is asked to "freeze". The group leader goes to each person while they are still in role and asks the character for one word, sentence, sound or gesture to describe how they are feeling in role at this moment.

# Physical de-roling

continued from previous page

## Washing away the role

Having removed the obvious signs of the dramatic roles, group members take an imaginary shower to symbolize physically letting go of their roles. Everyone mimes turning on a tap above their heads. They imagine the water cascading over their bodies and use their hands to show how it flows over the body and away. They make refreshing noises as if enjoying an invigorating shower. Some participants may like to 'scrub' the role off, making firmer contact with the whole body. This ritualized way of letting go of a role can become a regular group activity at the end of an enactment.

## Further development

Participants choose a partner to help wash away the role from behind (see 'Standing Massage', p. 53).

## Shaking off the role

A vigorous way of coming out of role and into the here and now reality is to shake the role off. Group members are invited to use the whole body, starting with the hands and arms, then including legs, feet, pelvis and back. Finally, they make sure the role is shaken from the head and face. The whole sequence should be accompanied by spontaneous sounds, using the voice to enhance the process. This exercise is also an energy raiser, useful when group energy is flagging.

## Blowing away the role

This can be used to follow washing away or shaking off a role. Each person gently blows their own body, feeling the breath on their skin. They begin with hands and arms, then try blowing their own faces, then over the shoulders and down the legs. The exercise is gentle but quite challenging, requiring concentration and flexibility to direct the breath to as many parts of the body as possible.

## Stepping out of the role

After a moment of stopping the action with the instruction to "freeze", the group leader invites the participants to step out of the skin of the character

# Physical de-roling

they have been playing and to return to their own selves. They imagine the role as a banana skin that can be peeled off in mime, from above the head down to the feet from several sides. When the banana skin is peeled down, everyone takes a deep breath, followed by a big step out. To ensure that they are back in their own skins they all tap, stroke and squeeze themselves.

The idea of the skin of a role can be carried forward into a discussion phase of de-roling (see 'Reflective De-roling', below). Everyone carries their imaginary banana skin into the centre of a circle, where the whole group can sit and give verbal feedback about what it was like to be in that role.

DE-ROLING 12

# Reflective de-roling

It is not always easy for people with learning difficulties to reflect on a process they have experienced and to verbalize their responses. One of the aims of de-roling is to create some distance and sense of relationship between 'me as me' and 'me as the role'. There follow some structures that give form to this process, making it more concrete and accessible.

## Group story

Sitting in a circle, group members put together their different experiences in the enactment. The action is repeated, in the form of a story. There are several approaches, depending on how articulate the group is and the level of independence of the participants.

### Talking stick round

- The group leader holds a maraca or talking stick and begins with the words, "One day. . .". The stick is passed around the circle and each person adds their part of the story when they have the talking stick.

### Talking stick at random

- A volunteer takes the talking stick and starts the story. When someone else is ready to continue they wave and the stick is passed to them. This continues until the story is completed.

### Eliciting the story

- The group leader elicits the key points of the story by asking questions which volunteers from the group fill in with a word or phrase. Questions include "Where did our story take place?" "Who was there?" "What were they doing?" "Then what happened?" "Were they happy about that?" and so on. At the end, group members are asked to suggest a title for the story.

## Similarities and differences

Ask the group to think about the role they have played in the enactment. What kind of character was it? One at a time, each person tries to identify something they have in common with that character, and something they do not have in common. The group leader can help with questions, such as

# Reflective de-roling

"How was it for you to play the part of the grumpy old man?", "Do you know what it is like to feel grumpy?" and "The man you played was old. How old are you?" Other group members can also help find examples of similarity and difference, focusing on each person in turn.

## Non-verbal role feedback

Each person thinks about the role they played in the enactment and makes a gesture or movement that describes the role. The way the movement is performed may suggest how the performer felt about playing the character. The group leader can reflect back verbally what she has seen. For example, "Yes, as the lion you snarled, growled and pounced. It looks like you really enjoyed that. Did you?"

## Further development

The whole group echoes or mirrors the gesture or movement made by each individual. Having felt the response physically, group members may suggest a word or image evoked by the movement.

## Interview

The group leader uses a microphone, or a talking stick as a microphone, to conduct a television-style interview with the various group members. Everyone talks into the microphone, so it is clear where the action and attention are centred. The group leader asks an individual questions, such as "What was your favourite moment in the story?" or "How did you feel when the gangsters burst into the bank?" Each person can be introduced as if to a television audience, to build up excitement. For example: "And now, ladies and gentlemen, it is my pleasure to introduce you to the man who played the policeman. . . a big welcome to Mike." At the end of each short interview, the interviewer gives formal thanks and creates a bridge to the whole group as audience saying, for instance, "Many thanks, Mike. Fascinating story, wasn't it?" At the end of the round of interviews, the interviewer says goodbye as if to a wider audience and the whole group applauds as at the end of a television broadcast.

# Reflective de-roling

*continued from previous page*

## Drawing a picture

At the end of an enactment, after coming back together as a group everyone draws a picture. This can represent a core moment in the story, the setting where it took place or the role they played. If this technique is repeated regularly, the number of pictures grows into a collection, providing a self-made record of the group's work over time. Group members may choose to exhibit this to a wider audience, or to use it as a private memory jogger for themselves. When a sequence of sessions comes to an end, such pictures can also help group members recollect key moments of their collective experience.

# 13

# Closures

# Closures

## Goodbye song

Following a similar principle to that of a hello song, a goodbye song gives a chance for the group to engage in a familiar whole-group activity that mentions each person by name. For example:

*Goodbye Tomas*
*Goodbye Tomas*
*Goodbye Tomas*
*We'll see you here next week!*

- This is repeated until all the names have been sung, including those of the group leaders. As each name is sung, everyone can look at that person and wave. The final verse refers to the whole group and is a reminder of the next session.

*Goodbye everyone*
*Goodbye everyone*
*Goodbye everyone*
*We'll see you here next week!*

## Goodbye dance

This activity expresses physically the processes of coming together as a group and then returning to an individual identity.

### Activity
The group stands in a large circle, holding hands. All move in towards the centre of the circle while raising their arms. They look at each other. From this stretch position they begin to move backwards, still holding hands, and lowering their arms. The movement is performed three times; the third time, group members make the stretch as full as possible and, as the circle expands again, let go hands so that each person stands independently. The group can devise sounds to accompany the movements. The group leader can talk through the exercise, emphasizing the coming together and the letting go, perhaps until the next session.

# Closures

*continued from previous page*

## Rhythmic build-up and wind-down

This exercise can be done using hands and body, voice or musical instruments. It demands concentration and listening skills.

### Activity

The group sits in a circle. One person begins a simple rhythm or sound which they repeat. They can clap hands, slap their knees or the floor, shake a maraca or sing a rhythmic phrase. Once this sound is established, the next person adds their own rhythm or sound, which they repeat. Gradually, one by one, everyone adds their sound. Then the wind-down begins. One at a time, in reverse order, each person stops, until only the first rhythm and sound remain. The pattern of the exercise involves a gradual crescendo, then a diminuendo, and finally an audible silence.

## Group shout

This is particularly useful when the energy is low at the end of a session. It engages the body and breath and does not require too much concentration.

### Activity

Stand in a circle. After a countdown from three to one, everyone shouts, "Goodbye!" as loudly as possible. Try it three times, getting louder each time and using the arms to help send the sound up and out. Then try a silent "Goodbye!" using eye contact and mouthing the word without using the voice.

## Meditation hum

This closure is pleasant after a very active session. It creates a soothing atmosphere and helps individuals to feel centred before leaving the group.

### Activity

Sit comfortably in a circle on chairs which are close enough to allow everyone to hold hands. Encourage everyone to sit with a straight back and to feel their feet placed firmly on the floor. All hold hands and close their eyes. Everyone is invited to hum to the sound 'Mm' and after a while to let this develop into an 'Aah' sound. The exact notes do not matter – the main thing

# Closures

is to listen to the sound of the group as a whole, to breathe and to vocalize. After a while; let the singing come to an end and sit for a few moments in silence, feeling the connection with the group and breathing softly. Finally, everyone opens their eyes.

## Pass the squeeze activity

Sit in a circle on the floor or on chairs. Hold hands. The group leader gives her neighbour on one side two squeezes to the rhythm of the word 'goodbye'. She can say the word 'goodbye' as well. This other person does the same with her other hand to her neighbour, and so on until the squeeze has come full circle. If this works, try it again with the eyes closed and in silence, relying only on the sense of touch.

## Goodbye gesture

This is a physical way of saying goodbye and allows each person the chance to make an individual contribution which is recognized by the group.

### Activity

Stand in a circle. One at a time, each person finds a non-verbal way to say goodbye to the group. This may be a traditional wave, a more formal bow or an abstract movement. The group focuses on each person in turn and responds by returning the gesture.

# 14

# Evaluation
# and creating an
# evidence base

# Evaluation and creating an evidence base

## Introduction

How do we know that our work in creative drama is effective? This is a question that will be of interest to anyone who is facilitating a creative drama group. From the point of view of managers, commissioners and care co-ordinators the question is particularly important as it can make the difference between continuing to provide the resources for such an activity or not.

When we are working with people with learning difficulties, who sometimes face multiple challenges, change tends to be slower to manifest, and we need to adjust our expectations of 'success' to meet the individual and participant group. It may be only when we look back after a significant period of work that we can see what achievements have been made.

I recommend keeping a note of each session, in terms of both content and process. These notes should be reviewed from time to time and a summary of group and individual achievements made.

There follow some simple ways to approach the task of creating both ongoing notes and an evidence base. Some of these are based on self-report of the participants, others depend on some observation of facilitators and group leaders as well as others involved in the care or education of the participants. Managers are encouraged to allow regular time for reflection and completion of the documentation for these evaluation tasks.

1  Session notes template. This will help to provide a record of engagement and achievements of the creative drama group.

# Evaluation and creating an evidence base

*continued from previous page*

## Session notes template

### Creative drama groupwork session notes template

This template can either be copied and filled in session by session, or used as a basis for creating your own template for process notes.

| |
|---|
| Date and session number: |
| Facilitated by: |
| Assisted by: |
| Location: |
| Time: |
| Group members expected: |
| Present: |
| Late: |
| Absent (and reason for absence): |

| |
|---|
| Session plan summary: |
| Arrivals and greetings: |
| Warm-up: |
| Development/main activity: |
| Distancing and de-roling: |
| Goodbyes and departures: |

# Evaluation and creating an evidence base

## Individual participant notes

| Name: | Participation in arrivals<br><br>Participation in warm-up<br><br>Participation in Development/main activity Participation in distancing and de-roling<br><br>Participation in goodbyes | |
|---|---|---|
| | Process notes (e.g., new challenges met, roles taken, engagement with peers, difficulties encountered) | |
| | What did they enjoy? Highlights | |
| | Difficulties encountered | |
| | How were these difficulties handled? | |
| Notes to self/carers/team | | |

# Evaluation and creating an evidence base

• • • • • • • • • • • • • • • • • • • • • • • • • • • • • • • • • • • • • •

*continued from previous page*

**2** Sociometry self-report evaluation notes. This will help to provide a record of changes over time, and what activities different individuals engaged with or struggled with.

## Sociometry self-report form

### Sociometry self-report evaluation notes for creative drama groupwork

Sociometry is a method of measuring responses through action. You can devise your own ways of building up an evidence. Here are some starting points.

Method 1: Investigating mood at start and end of session. This only takes a moment and can be seen as part of the warm up and closure for the session.

All together, raise an arm up high for 10 – I'm feeling great right now

Way down low for 1 – I'm feeling lousy

Somewhere in the middle – 5 I'm okay, not great, but could be worse.

Variation: Move to this end of the room to represent I'm feeling great now, the other end of the room to represent I'm feeling lousy and somewhere in the middle to represent I'm okay, not great, but could be worse.

Group report for session number.... On date....

| Start of the session | Good mood – how many? | Neutral – how many? | Low mood – how many? | Notes |
|---|---|---|---|---|
| End of the session | Good mood – how many? | Neutral – how many? | Low mood – how many? | Notes |

CREATIVE DRAMA GROUPWORK FOR PEOPLE WITH LEARNING DIFFICULTIES

# Evaluation and creating an evidence base

Method 2 Self-evaluation of session activities

Step into the circle if you agree with the following statements – the examples below should be substituted with the actual activities of the session:

| Activity | Statement | How many stepped in? | How many stayed out? | Notes |
|---|---|---|---|---|
| Newsround | I really enjoyed the newsround today | | | |
| The name–place game | I liked playing the game | | | |
| The vocal orchestra | I liked doing the orchestra | | | |

The observations of the facilitator and team within the session are also of value in creating an evidence base. It is important to have time to reflect on the session notes taken after each session and to make some sense of them. I advocate doing this as a reflective team exercise, leading towards the creation of a report for the group as a whole and for all individual participants.

These are some of the goals for a creative drama group taken from the Introduction to this book:

**Once in a while (termly, annually or at the end of a short project) the staff team and participants can reflect on the extent to which these goals have been achieved.**

# Evaluation and creating an evidence base

• • • • • • • • • • • • • • • • • • • • • • • • • • • • • • • • • • • • • • • • • • •

*continued from previous page*

Take some time individually as facilitator or as a team to reflect on each of these and note down one or two examples where you feel the group and individuals in the group have achieved the goal.

1 helping a group to bond (notice co-operation between group members, pleasure at meeting in the context of the group, willingness to engage with each other in activities)

2 increasing tolerance, respect and understanding between group members (notice small informal exchanges between group members, any changes in expressions of impatience or irritation with each other, willingness to help)

3 enhancing individual self-esteem and the confidence to communicate (notice willingness to take a central position, to adopt a role, or actively make a suggestion or choice)

4 increasing the awareness and appreciation of boundaries, physical, social and emotional (notice changing ability to engage with the rules of a game or structure, to stay present in activities, to tolerate not being the centre of attention, to turn-take)

5 developing social skills (notice appropriate and less appropriate communication styles, and how these may change over time)

6 developing physical skills (notice expressiveness, mobility, flexibility, control, spontaneity)

7 developing verbal skills (notice any increase in active expression through words, and passive demonstration of verbal understanding through action)

8 developing assertiveness, self-advocacy and life skills (notice moments of choice making within the group and any applied life skills from outside reported within the group)

9 developing spontaneity (particularly for the quieter or more reserved group members notice increased readiness to try something new, be heard or seen)

CREATIVE DRAMA GROUPWORK FOR PEOPLE WITH LEARNING DIFFICULTIES

# Evaluation and creating an evidence base

10 enhancing the ability to make choices (notice the choices made within different drama structures)

11 developing the imagination and the ability to play (notice participation in games, role plays and dramatizations)

12 learning about other people, places and times beyond the immediate here and now (notice interest in the drama structures and discussions arising out of these).

# Further reading

Andersen-Warren M, *Creative Groupwork with Elderly People: Drama*, Winslow Press/Speechmark, 1997.

Astell-Burt C, *Puppetry for Mentally Handicapped People*, Souvenir Press, 1981.

Bailey S D, *Wings to Fly, Bringing Theatre Arts to Students with Special Needs*, Woodbine House, 1993.

Chesner A, 'An integrated model of dramatherapy and its application with adults with learning disabilities', in Jennings, S, Cattanach, A, Mitchell, S, Chesner, A, & Meldrum, B. *The Handbook of Dramatherapy*, Routledge, 1994.

Chesner A, *Dramatherapy for People with Learning Disabilities, A World of Difference*, Jessica Kingsley, 1995.

Delaney T, *101 Games and Activities for Children with Autism, Asperger's and Sensory Processing Disorders*, McGraw-Hill Education, 2009.

Gersie A, *Storymaking in Education and Therapy*, Jessica Kingsley Publishers, 1989.

Haythorne D & Seymour A (eds), *Dramatherapy and Autism*, Routledge, 2016.

Hickson A, *The Groupwork Manual*, Winslow Press/Speechmark, 1997.

Hodgson J & Richards E, *Improvisation*, Methuen, 1966.

Jennings S, *Remedial Drama*, Pitman, 1973.

Jennings S, *Role-Play Cards for Social Skills*, Winslow Press/Speechmark, 1988.

Jennings S, *Healthy Attachments and Neuro-Dramatic-Play*, Jessica Kingsley Publishers, 2010.

Jennings S, *Creative Drama in Groupwork* (second edition), Routledge, 2010.

Langley D, *An Introduction to Dramatherapy (Creative Therapies in Practice Series)*, Sage, 2006.

McCurrach I & Darnley B, *Special Talents, Special Needs*, Jessica Kingsley, 1999.

Payne H, *Creative Movement & Dance in Groupwork* (second edition), Routledge, 2019.

# Further reading

continued from previous page

**Pearson J, Smail M & Watts P,** *Dramatherapy with Myth and Fairytale: The Golden Stories of Sesame,* Jessica Kingsley, 2013.

**Perich Carleton J,** *Story Drama in the Special Needs Classroom: Step-by-Step Lesson Plans for Teaching through Dramatic Play,* Jessica Kingsley Publishers, 2012.

**Sherborne V,** *Developmental Movement for Children: Mainstream, Special Needs and Pre-School,* Cambridge University Press, 1990.

**Sonnet H & Taylor A,** *Activities for Adults with Learning Disabilities: Having Fun, Meeting Needs,* Jessica Kingsley Publishers, 2009.

**Spolin V,** *Improvisation for the Theatre: A Handbook of Teaching and Directing Techniques,* Northwestern University Press, 1983.

**Sunderland M,** *Using Story Telling as a Therapeutic Tool with Children,* Speechmark, 2001.

**Thomas D & Woods H,** *Working with People with Learning Disabilities: Theory and Practice,* Jessica Kingsley, 2003.

# Index

................................................

# Index

●●●●●●●●●●●●●●●●●●●●●●●●●●●●●●●●●●●●●●●●●●●●●●●●●●●●●●●●●●

*continued from previous page*